Additional Praise for *Balsamic Dreams*

"A sardonic, often laugh-out-loud puncturing of Baby Boomer pretensions . . . A scathing dissection of the lamest generation in all their latte-loving vainglory."
—*Kirkus Reviews* (starred review)

"Joe Queenan is a guilty pleasure, an anger artist who is so funny that your better angels take flight as he sweeps you away in his comic cruelty. . . . Though we've heard it all before, no one has said it better. When Queenan's poison pen is flowing, his put-downs sound like aphorisms, what Poor Richard might have said on a really bad day."
—J. Peder Zane, *The News & Observer* (Raleigh, North Carolina)

"A hilarious, quasi-maniacal extended rant against the Baby Boomers. You'd think Queenan's own membership in that much-maligned demographic would make him soften his critique, but he pulls no punches—proving that at least some Boomers are capable of self-criticism."
—Maria Russo, Salon.com

"Queenan . . . dissects these ephemeral creatures as delicately as an entomologist examining the inner workings of a mayfly. He lays bare their failings, foibles, fatuities, flaws, and fads with a keen and unsentimental knife. The pages bristle with caustic wit and deadly parody . . . a fully diverting diversion."
—*Library Journal*

"A hilarious send-up . . . Queenan's cranky writing is stand-up-comedy funny."
—*Seattle Post-Intelligencer*

"In English dictionaries of the future, under the word 'curmudgeon,' we are highly likely to find Joe Queenan's mug. Whether taking on sacred cows or mad-cow disease, Queenan is the boy wonder of nihilistic criticism."
—Mary Welp, *Louisville Courier-Journal*

"The king of kvetch shoots another riotous round out of his canon. . . . As always, Queenan's rants work like a colonic cleanser on such deadly toxins as 'tasteful self-absorption.'" —Kristin Tillotson, *Minneapolis Star Tribune*

"Anyone even vaguely familiar with the exploits of a generation that Queenan has christened 'the most obnoxious people in the history of the human race' will savor every page of this alternately cranky and deadly accurate cross-examination." —Rob Stout, *Atlanta Journal-Constitution*

"If you've ever had to listen to the Boomers rhapsodizing about their idyllic youth—and who among us has escaped this torture?—all you can say after reading *Balsamic Dreams* is: Amen." —Jeremy Lott, *The Weekly Standard*

"Joe Queenan is America's preeminent wisenheimer. . . . Queenan endures Boomers as he would itchy underpants; his readers have the luxury of sharing his crabbiness without feeling his pain." —John Rezek, *Playboy*

"A hysterical, read-in-one-sitting indictment of a generation." —James Marrow, *The National Review*

"[A] witty, sardonic, and heartfelt paean to his fellow aging Boomers." —*Publishers Weekly*

BALSAMIC
DREAMS

BALSAMIC DREAMS

A Short but

Self-Important

History of

the Baby Boomer

Generation

JOE QUEENAN

Picador USA
Henry Holt and Company
New York

www.picadorusa.com

Picador® is a U.S. registered trademark and is used by Henry Holt and Company under license from Pan Books Limited.

For information on Picador USA Reading Group Guides, as well as ordering, please contact the Trade Marketing department at St. Martin's Press.
Phone: 1-800-221-7945 extension 763
Fax: 212-677-7456
E-mail: trademarketing@stmartins.com

Library of Congress Cataloging-in-Publication Data

Queenan, Joe.
    Balsamic dreams : a short but self-important history of the baby boomer generation / Joe Queenan.
        p. cm.
    ISBN 0-312-42082-X
    1. Baby boom generation—United States. 2. United States—Social conditions—1945– 3. United States—Social life and customs—1971– I. Title.

HN57 .Q44 21
305.24—dc21   00-054248

First published in the United States by Henry Holt and Company

First Picador USA Edition: June 2002

10 9 8 7 6 5 4 3 2 1

To Joe and Mary Weiss

Contents

- -

Prologue

Late in the summer of the year of our Lord 2000, I began to suffer from a nagging cough. Although it was entirely possible that the cough was the result of hay fever, the naturally downbeat cast of my personality already had me thinking more in terms of lung cancer. Confronted by my own mortality, I began to lament all the things I had not yet accomplished with my life.

True, I had written a book (several, in fact), planted a tree and sired a son, so masculine-rites-of-passage-wise I was way ahead of the game. But I had never seen the Taj Mahal, never meandered along the Great Wall of China, never glimpsed, much less scaled, Mount Everest, never stood transfixed scant paces from a white lion on the plains of the Serengeti, never snorkled in the piranha-infested narrows of the Amazon, never planted my feet at the North Pole and watched a polar bear gently cuff her naughty cubs. Forty-nine years old and fast approaching fifty, I had let my life slip away from me and was now forced to admit how poorly I had prepared myself for death.

The very next day, I started taking piano lessons. It was something I'd been wanting to do for a long time, anyway, but now that I could hear Time's winged hoofbeats clattering up the driveway, it seemed like a good time to get cracking on the old eighty-eights. At the same time, I started reading Marcel Proust's *Remembrance of Things Past* and Edward Gibbon's *Decline and Fall of the Roman Empire* because I didn't want to die without having polished off that internal reading list everyone in my general age group carries around inside him. I also signed up for a cooking class, arranged to have a flying lesson at a nearby airport, and made serious inquiries about enrolling in a local tai chi class. And even though there was every reason to believe that I was dying, I stopped by the YMCA and looked into securing the services of a personal trainer. Just because I was getting ready to meet my Maker didn't mean it was too late to get myself back into fighting trim. Besides, I wanted to look sharp at the funeral.

I now confided in a friend that I was imminently headed gently into that good night, and asked if he had any suggestions about how to handle my personal swan song. While we were discussing funeral arrangements, he asked where I would like to have my ashes scattered. "What are my options?" I inquired. I had several, he explained. For starters, I could go the obvious route and have my ashes wafted to the four winds in the city of my birth, Philadelphia, which would give my passing a certain municipal resonance, a subtle variation on the old be-true-to-your-school refrain.

But the Schuylkill and the Delaware are not exactly mythic waterways, and they are certainly not in the same league as the Ganges or the Nile, where the tasteful integration of one's remains into the ecosystem might certify that one had finally arrived, in the karmic sense of the word, albeit not under the best of circumstances. And since I had spent half my life in New York and its environs, scattering my ashes in the City of Brotherly Love seemed both biographically and ecologically suspect.

Conversely, dispersing my ashes into the Hudson or the East River wouldn't do the trick either. True, I had lived in the New York metropolitan area for twenty-four years. But like so many other semi-rustics who had come to the big city seeking fame and fortune, I had never stopped feeling that I was only passing through. Much as I loved New York, I never got the impression that it loved me back. It was too busy hating Los Angeles. Moreover, the Hudson and the East Rivers are grungy cesspools, where my ashes would get mixed in with a lot of PCBs and rat hair. All in all, this idea seemed kind of gross.

In the end, my friend advised me to play things safe and upscale by consigning my ashes to the Seine. Since I had lived in Paris as a young man, and since it was my favorite place in the whole wide world, and since my childhood heroes Henry Miller, Peter Abelard, Molière, Ernest Hemingway, Oscar Wilde, Erasmus, F. Scott Fitzgerald, George Orwell, Louis XIV, the Marquis de Sade and Jim Morrison had all lived there at one time or another, I felt that entrusting my charred remains to the Seine would confer a piquant mythological legitimacy on my passing. And so it was decided.

After I'd taken care of the piano lessons and the tai chi and the personal trainer and the airplane lessons and made the relevant inquiries about a ceremonial trip to Kathmandu, I figured it was time that I got my wife and children up to speed, mortality-wise. Here I hit some rough sailing. Seeing that I had only just entered my prime earning years and that my career seemed to be going extraordinarily well after hitting a fiscal plateau in the mid-nineties, my wife was a little ticked off that I should have picked this time to die. She suggested that I seek a second opinion. With my son off at soccer camp and my daughter tied up with an ambitious high school xeno transplantation project, I didn't get a chance to broach the subject right away. Which is just as well, because when I did finally get the cough checked out, it was diagnosed as a generic allergy attack, perhaps in response to New York's zero-tolerance West Nile virus spraying, but nothing requiring a trip to the funeral home.

Immensely relieved, I dropped the piano and cooking lessons, put off learning to fly an airplane, stuck the trip to the Inscrutable Orient on the back burner and jammed Marcel Proust back up there on the bookshelf with all those unread Robert Musil and Italo Calvino novels. I also informed my friend that on his next visit to Paris, he would have extra room in his luggage, as he would not be carrying my ashes.

That night, my sleep was deeply troubled. My brush with death, however fleeting, however absurd, had brought me face-to-face with my own most jealously guarded values and had unearthed a number of shocking inadequacies in my life. No, I was no longer regretting all the things I had yet to accomplish during my brief sojourn on the planet: learning Catalan, clambering up the steps of Machu Picchu, visiting every baseball stadium in the United States of America, owning a seat on the Chicago Board of Trade. Instead, I was realizing how revoltingly venal and self-centered my reaction to the specter of death had been. I was subconsciously calibrating what an astoundingly selfish person I was. I was quietly coming to terms with the fact that, despite the lovingly crafted facade of charm, wit, sophistication and class that masqueraded as a personality, I was basically a worthless person.

Look how I had reacted to the thought that I might be dying of lung cancer. Did I say to myself "Now might be a good time to help eradicate poverty in rural America"? No. Did I ask myself "Wouldn't this be a good opportunity to spend some time in a leper colony?" No. Did I ask myself "Why not use your few remaining months to make this planet a better place than the way you found it?" Of course not.

Instead, I embarked on a mad binge of self-aggrandizement. Rather than capitalizing on my remaining days and weeks to reconcile myself to my enemies, spend more time with my loved ones, consult wise men regarding the meaning of life, I had succumbed to the siren song of self-actualization.

Yet, in my defense, I was not the only member of my age group who would have reacted in this way. For in choosing this pointless, self-involved course of action, I was, if nothing else, being true to the ethos of my generation. When faced with unsettling developments like death, Baby Boomers always react in the same way: We sign up for self-improvement classes. A Baby Boomer par excellence, a prototypical product of the Me Decade, I only knew how to respond to the world insofar as it responded to *moi*. Everything I had ever learned as a Baby Boomer had oriented me in a single direction: further into myself. Now I had to face the ugly truth, not only about me, but about us: We were appalling. We had appalling values. We had appalling taste. And one of the most appalling things about us was that we liked to use appalling words like "appalling."

As I took stock of my revolting personality, threadbare values and dessicated intellect, I was forced to admit that I had too long shielded my eyes from the horrid truth about my generation. We were duds. We had started off okay with the Freedom Riders and Woodstock and Four Dead in Ohio and driving Nixon from office and Jon Voight in *Midnight Cowboy* and so on. But then we hit a rough patch. We became crass and self-absorbed. We stopped caring about anything but money and food. We fell in love with our stereo equipment. We obsessed about our footwear. We wore garish Fu Manchus and culturally incongruous peasant dresses and acted like we were on to something.

We abandoned the poor, the downtrodden and the oppressed because we were doing postdoctoral work in American Studies. We acted like we were better than the proles because we knew how to spell "polenta." We made stars out of people like Rod Stewart and Billy Joel, and then, when called on the carpet to explain these outrages, we retreated behind the palisades of irony. We sent our kids to enrichment programs in paltry third-world countries, where they could observe the last bastions of socialism up close and personal, even though we were loading up on thirty-year treasuries. We signed on to every half-assed health fad that came down the pike, even though we were fast becoming fat drunks.

We didn't stop there. We made millionaires out of nitwits like Deepak Chopra and Tom Clancy while geniuses starved. We played air guitar and Rotisserie League Baseball in the fifteen-hundred-square-foot dens of our cookie-cutter McMansions and pretended that we were still street-fighting men ready to off the pigs. First we refused to grow up, and then when we were, technically speaking, *grown up*, we refused to admit it. We invented stupid verbs like "interface," "prioritize" and "parent," then turned them into stupid gerunds like "interfacing," "prioritizing" and "parenting." We dreamed up fantasy baseball camps where jock-sniffing asses could hang out with ass-kissing jocks. We made the *Eagles Greatest Hits* the best-selling U.S. album of all time, we foisted the Gipsy Kings on an unsuspecting society; we fell deeply in love with pseudo-ethnic hooey like *Riverdance* and *Angela's Ashes* and Kwanza, we subjected our cowering children to the unforgiving lash of ELO, the Dead and Tull. And all along, we acted like we were still really, really cool.

As the years went by, it became clear that our sellout was no mere fluke. Yet, through it all, I was silent. I saw some of my male colleagues put their hair up in ponytails as early as 1971, yet I was silent. I watched my friends heave their Three Dog Night records into the incinerator and slip the Three Tenors onto the CD player, yet I was silent. I watched friends who had been teargassed and billy-clubbed the day we levitated the Pentagon now trundle off for two weeks on Martha's Vineyard, where they could read both *Under the Tuscan Sun* and *Toujours Provence* while listening to Andrea Bocelli and the original-cast album from *Miss Saigon*, yet I was silent. I watched my friends sign checks to the Democratic party and then send their children to posh private schools, yet I was silent. I watched intransigent Maoists once ready to go to the wall in the cause of freedom now go to Wall Street in the cause of Chinese paper, yet I was silent. I watched an entire generation make its separate peace with society and console itself with useless cooking classes, counterproductive photography seminars, completely extraneous Portuguese lessons. Yet through it all, I was silent.

I can hold my tongue no longer.

Today, more in sorrow than in anger, I take my pen in hand. I undertake this project—more a cross-examination than an official history—as a way of atoning both for my sins and for the sins of my generation. For too long I have filled my coffers by ridiculing toothless seniors, hapless trailer trash, lunkheaded slackers. Always I have kept the stiletto sharpened; always I have pointed it away from my own generation. Now that stiletto is changing direction.

It is hard to say exactly what pushed me over the edge. Certainly, watching Tipper Gore perform that peculiar dance at the 2000 Democratic National Convention could not have helped. Yet when all is said and done, I undertake this task not because Tipper danced too much but because I danced too little. In taking this bold step, I recognize the dangers to myself, my family and my career. Some of my contemporaries will feel betrayed by my indictment. Some may feel that I have sold them down the river in the hope of currying favor with younger people well-positioned to affect my future. Some may call me a Benedict Arnold, a Judas Iscariot, an Et tu, Brute. To them I can only repeat the immortal words of E. M. Forster: "If I had to choose between betraying my country and betraying my friend, I hope I should have the guts to betray my country."

This is a nice sentiment, but I don't share it. If I had to choose between betraying my friends and betraying my country, I'd betray my friends in a heartbeat. We had a few good times together, smoked some fabulous reefer, listened to a couple of far-out, totally cosmic *Firesign Theater* records, but if you want the God's honest truth, Baby Boomers are the most obnoxious people in the history of the human race. Back in the sixties, we used to have a saying: "If you're not part of the solution, you're part of the problem."

For the first time in thirty years, I've decided to be part of the solution.

1

J'Accuse

Throughout history, generations imbued with a messianic complex have inspired a wide range of powerful emotions. The Jacobins who decapitated Louis XVI inspired dread. The insurgents led by George Washington inspired admiration. The twentysomething barbarians who accompanied Genghis Khan on his pitiless campaigns through Central Asia and Eastern Europe inspired despair, the young Germans who put Hitler's name in lights inspired horror, the fresh-faced Frenchmen and Frenchwomen who built the cathedrals of Chartres and Amiens and Beauvais inspired awe.

Baby Boomers fall into a somewhat different category. As convinced of their uniqueness as the Bolsheviks, as persuaded of their genius as the Victorians, as self-absorbed as the Romantics, as prosperous as the ancient Romans, the Baby Boomers, despite a very good start (the Freedom Riders, Woodstock, Four Dead in Ohio, driving Nixon from office, Jon Voigt in *Midnight Cowboy*), have never put many points on the historical scoreboard. Feared and admired in their youth, today they inspire little more than irritation. Not outright revulsion, not apoplectic fury, but simple, unadorned garden-variety irritation. With a bit of contempt thrown in on the side.

The single most damning, and obvious, criticism that can be leveled at Baby Boomers is, of course, that they promised they wouldn't sell out and become fiercely materialistic like their parents, and then they did. They further complicated matters by mulishly spending their entire adult lives trying to persuade themselves and everybody else that they had not in fact sold out, that they had merely matured and grown wiser, that their values had undergone some sort of benign intellectual mutation. This only made things worse, because they had now compounded the sin of avarice with the sin of deceit. Besides, it was useless to deny their monstrous cupidity; banks keep records of this sort of thing.

They had not been the first generation to sell out, but they were the first generation to sell out and then insist that they hadn't. Here was their central tragedy, the poisoned well from which all their unhappiness flowed. They were conflicted. They were flummoxed. Their center would not hold, because they were no longer centered.

They could not process the information that their guilt was misplaced, that no one in the United States of America would ever blame anyone for devoting every single moment of his life to the pursuit of filthy lucre—as long as he didn't try pretending that he hadn't. The heartbreak of the Baby Boomer generation lay in the fact that they could not fully enjoy the wealth they had moved heaven and earth to acquire because they felt tainted by their ravenous greed. Baby Boomers would have turned out so much saner and happier if they had ripped a page from the Founding Fathers' playbook and said, "Yes, I chopped down that cherry tree. And then I securitized it into four equal tranches, with the first two splices reverting to the underwriter. You got a problem with that?"

Clearly, this refusal to own up to their own acquisitiveness is not the Baby Boomers' only broken promise. They said they wouldn't become crass and vulgar. But they are. They said they would never become horrid conformists. But they are. They said they would not be ruthless materialists. But then they embraced a complete *Lifestyle Über Alles* philosophy, carping and caviling at dinner parties over which local bakery sold the best sourdough *boules*, which kayak shop offered the most attractive warranties, which brand of grappa was most culturally authentic. It was a generation that once prided itself on questioning authority. Now its only questions were referred to authorities like Williams-Sonoma: "Is *l'aceto di Modena* superior to *l'aceto di Reggio*? Is *Calasparra* or *arborio* rice more desirable in preparing *paella a la Valencia*?" Their utopian visions of peace, love and understanding had been replaced by balsamic dreams.

In the end, Baby Boomers didn't deliver on any of their promises. Instead, they were a case study in false advertising. They professed to go with the flow, but it was actually the cash flow, and they most certainly did not teach their children well, as they were too busy videotaping them. Instead, they took a dive. They retreated into the deepest recesses of their surprisingly tiny inner lives. They became fakes, hypocrites, cop-outs and, in many cases, out-and-out dorks. And the worst thing was: Most of them didn't realize it.

CERTAINLY NOT MR. Dog Guy. One day last summer I was sitting on the veranda of my elegant, well-appointed house overlooking the Hudson River when a Jeep Grand Cherokee drifted past with a twee Alaskan malamute trotting about twenty yards behind. As the Jeep inched up the street at about five miles an hour, the dog meekly scurried along in its wake, occasionally soiling people's lawns. The dog and the vehicle soon disappeared around a bend in the road, but five minutes later they were back for the return leg of their little jaunt. When the dog attempted to do his business on my wife's beloved flower bed, I made it my business to scare him away with a stick. The dog clambered off and that was that.

Over the course of the next three weeks, I observed the Jeep and the dog making their rounds early in the morning and late in the evening. The driver, about forty-five, was not from the neighborhood. Neither was the dog. The dog usually had the good sense to stay away from my lawn, but he invariably managed to take a dump somewhere else. The two quickly became a kind of local legend. Everyone felt sorry for a pet unlucky enough to have an owner who was too lazy to get out of his car and actually walk the poor mutt. Everyone wondered what kind of a creep would own a beautiful dog like that and not only refuse to walk it, but refuse to clean up after it, and who would then compound that offense by driving to someone else's neighborhood and encouraging his dog to defecate all over strangers' properties. My neighbors proclaimed him a creep, a lowlife, a swine, not to mention a very thoughtless and insensitive human being.

All this he was. But he was more, much more. I had often seen Dog Guy yammering away on his understatedly elegant cell phone in his fully loaded vehicle while multitasking his debonair trophy dog—and I knew exactly who he was. He was a consummate Baby Boomer, the kind of person who was too busy to get out of his car and walk his dog because his time was too valuable. Without a doubt, Dog Guy had conducted a costs-benefits analysis and decided that he would lose more money climbing down from the car and walking the dog than if he stayed inside on the phone talking to his broker, his personal trainer, his mistress.

Eventually, Dog Guy and Dog stopped coming around. Lusting after fresh conquests, they had no doubt invaded another unsuspecting village. Or perhaps hired a live-in bilingual dog-sitter—yes, at roughly the same time, I had seen an ad seeking the services of just such a person on the bulletin board of my local laundromat. Yet the memory of those three weeks lingers to this day, for in the capricious behavior of this individual I first recognized an important truth: that before the Baby Boomer Era, this sort of nation-wide sociopathic behavior had never existed. It is true that throughout our history, there had always been uncouth people who thought they were better than everybody else, people who had decided at an early age that the rules did not apply to them. But they were invariably rich people, so it was possible to attribute most of their baronial incivility to decades of inbreeding. Moreover, they were never terri-bly numerous and rarely came into direct contact with ordinary citizens.

This is what makes the Baby Boomers different: They're stupefyingly self-centered, unbelievably rude, obnoxious beyond belief, and they're everywhere. Until the rise of Baby Boomers, America only had to deal with a few thousand geographically spaced people who acted like pigs. Now it has millions of them. This is the downside of prosperity.

The adventures of Dog Guy, underscoring not only the failings of my generation but also my own shortcomings as a human being, finally moved me to take a stand. How did I intend to do this? After studious reflection, I decided to draw up a formal indictment of my generation. It seemed that someone should try to get all of our crimes down on paper so that future generations could use it as evidence against us and also learn from our mistakes. In this sense I was preparing an amicus curiae brief for our children and the children of our children, mindful of Cokie Roberts's astute observation that we are all our mothers' daughters. And, by extension, our fathers' sons. And our grandpar-ents' grandchildren. And so on and so forth.

In preparing this indictment, I have tried to stick closely to crimes that any sensible person of any other generation would find actionable, and not merely indulge in personal vendettas against people I despise, like Ben & Jerry. Wherever possible, I have endeavored to avoid invoking such nonspecific terms as "lameness," for lameness is an almost universal Baby Boomer characteristic and by definition incorporates many of the accusations contained herein. I have attempted to enumerate attitudes as well as actions, thoughts as well as words. And I have also recorded quite a few pertinent observations about attire. If I have omitted any high crimes of which Baby Boomers have been found guilty as charged, I apologize in advance. But I don't think I have. Here then is a list of the essential habits, values, neuroses, prejudices, blind spots, fashion notions and idiosyncrasies that make Baby Boomers so thoroughly unbearable.

The cult of the tyke. The way Baby Boomers "parent" their menacingly precocious children is less child worship than devil worship. They simply cannot accept that children are only sources of pleasure to the two—or, in the case of Melissa Etheridge, three—people who brought them into the world, and usually only because those in question hope to one day convert them into animate revenue-generating streams.

True, it is probably unfair to hate the child accessory just because it is named Jenna, Jared, Josh, Jason or Jordan and started studying Manchurian aikido and the oud at age two. But then again, how can one not? Baby Boomers, by spawning children so vile they could give that kid in

The Omen a run for his money, have put the rest of society in the awkward position of wanting to see children who have not yet attained the age of reason put to the sword.

In many cases, these children don't have a prayer to begin with; since birth they've been groomed as stalking-horses for their parents, who have handcrafted them in their own odious images. A friend of mine runs a fine suburban restaurant. It serves traditional American cuisine in a traditional American setting. Its walls are adorned with old paintings, posters, bric-a-brac. Most patrons find it charming. One day, a family arrived for lunch. They seemed harmless enough. After the meal, the parents approached the owner of the restaurant and announced that their ominously pert ten-year-old daughter had something to say. The owner hoped the girl would compliment her on the peach cobbler or the Cajun chicken. She did not.

Instead, pointing to a mounted deer's head high on the wall, the girl proclaimed, "I think it's disgusting that you have that poor animal's head hanging from the wall." She then departed, accompanied by her proud, beaming, morally reenergized parents, fresh from a bracing midday catharsis.

Here we have the nuclear Baby Boomer family at its most repulsive. First off, we are in the presence of the precocious child, wise beyond her years, possibly as a result of the colorful, oversize Heisenberg Uncertainty Principle flash cards to which she was exposed as an infant. Second, we are confronted by the voluble child, oblivious to the time-honored dictum that children should be seen and not heard. (In deploring the cult of the child, Andy Ferguson of *The Weekly Standard* once observed that if small children knew so much, how come we didn't put them in charge of the Federal Reserve?) Third, we find ourselves crossing swords with the diplomatically protected child who is smart enough to realize that if she expressed her opinions to the owner of a busy, crowded restaurant sans parental aegis, the owner would probably jam her opinionated little mug into the Ligurian Pansotti with Walnut Pesto. Provided it was the special that day.

But in the end, it is the parents who must be blamed for the satanic exploits of their loathsome progeny. And in this vignette, we witness numerous components of the Baby Boomer psyche. For starters, always pick a fight you know you can't lose, in this case because the restaurant owner is unlikely to tell your kid to go screw herself. (It is amazing how rarely one hears of a Baby Boomer family bursting into a rural Arkansas roadhouse and demanding that the owner tear down the Confederate flag because it is offensive to African-Americans.) Next, try to seize the moral high ground in a situation where your target isn't even aware of the moral law he has transgressed. (It wasn't the restaurant owner who shot, beheaded and mounted the deer, and it's not like this was the only commercial establishment in the country with a deer's head on the wall.) Finally, wherever possible make use of the tried-and-true Proxy Attack, by assigning your kid the role of Child Javert because you don't have the guts to do it yourselves, you tragic wieners.

Quality time. Master of the Universe dads spend an hour a day with their children and expect to be awarded the Croi de Guerre. Juggler Boomer moms make teddy bear pancakes once every four years and expect a ticker-tape parade down Broadway. Whenever some fatuous journalist wants to make a point about what a superb, well-rounded individual some villainous plutocrat or hideous journalist is, he always mentions that the person takes off every Friday afternoon to go to his son's baseball game or to take his daughter ice-skating. So did Lucky Luciano. Maybe it's true that the Boomers spend a lot of time with their families, but so did the Borgias and the House of Atreus.

The unseemly search for the Fountain of Youth. It has always been possible for a small number of people to remain cool well into middle age (think Cary Grant, David Bowie, Samuel Beckett, Katharine Hepburn). But it has never been possible for a large number to do so. Harrison Ford showing off his naked chest in three consecutive movies (*Six Days and Seven Nights, Random Hearts, What Lies Beneath*) is a perfect example of Baby Boomers' refusing to accept the passage of time. *No, the earring will not help. No, the* Stones big tongue *T-shirt actually dates you. And please do something about that spiky hair; Halloween is still six months away.*

The concept of the "statement." It started with statement buttons ("Dylan Is Divine," "Proust Is a Yenta"), then spread to statement hair, statement clothing and statement drugs. But before long it spread to everything. Ultimately, there were statement houses, statement cars, statement motorcycles, statement bicycles, statement mountain bicycles, statement appliances, statement dogs, statement children, statement adopted children, statement names for statement adopted (a.k.a. "pre-parented") children. There were also statement wives, who differed from trophy wives in that they did not have to be young or beautiful; indeed, their preposterous hideousness could be an integral part of the statement. There were statement ties, statement shirts, statement footwear, statement bumper stickers, statement magazines, statement graves, statement gyms, statement diseases, statement CD collections. Statements have become so ubiquitous in this society that when people go out of their way to avoid wearing clothing bearing any kind of message or logo, they are only doing it to make a statement about statements.

Never-ending self-reference. Baby Boomers act like no one else has ever heard of Baby Boomers. So they constantly have to broadcast obvious autobiographical data like "I campaigned for McGovern" or "I got teargassed during the 1971 antiwar protests" or "I used to go out with a Puerto Rican girl who touched my perfect body with her mind when I was at Oberlin." Actually, the rest of American society knows this particular drill. They've been hearing it since 1968. They may not believe every sacred shard of this arcane mythology, but they know it. By heart.

The edgy-maverick paradox. A couple of years ago, I wrote a story for *Forbes* in which I blasted Paul Allen and David Geffen and Larry Ellison and all the rest of those populist plutocrats for playing air guitar or wearing gym clothes or appearing barefoot in magazine photographs. They were all billionaires many times over, but they wanted to portray themselves as *rock 'n' roll* billionaires. They wanted to show the Great Unwashed that they could *get down*. Sorry, guys, not this millennium. Each and every one of you is Babbit Redux, the Man in the Gray Flannel Track Suit.

At its heart, the disjointed feelings of billionaires about their own ersatz coolness offers a glimpse of the fundamental Baby Boomer problem writ large. How do I sell pork belly futures by day yet still keep that *Diamond Dogs* edge by night? The answer: You can't. You made your bed, now lie in it, sahib. The boots, the bike, the beard, the Buddhism—they're only going to confuse the kids.

As every generation in every society in the history of mankind has had to learn, much to its sorrow, trying to stay cool long after it is desirable—much less feasible—is undignified and sad. This is particularly true of what the French refer to as *l'hipster de droite* (the right-wing hep-cat), who dresses in *le style vieux jeune homme* (old young-guy wear). The frantic attempt by roly-poly middle-aged Republicans to evince an aura of coolness because they possess one (1) Smashing Pumpkins record and two (2) suede jackets with virtually imperceptible leopard spots is utterly unbecoming. It is not now, nor has it ever been, possible for middle-aged Republicans to be cool. This is, after all, the party of Lincoln. Remember *that* look?

The passing of the cosmic buck. Baby Boomers like to take credit for everything good that has happened to this society in the past three decades, but invariably blame anonymous miscreants or wayfaring strangers for everything bad. The civil rights movement, the Beatles, the ouster of Richard Nixon, the Rolling Stones, the rise of feminism, Jimi Hendrix, increased racial tolerance, Janis Joplin, a dramatic drop in the number of lynchings in the rural south, Creedence, a lightening-up of society in general, and the first two Allman Brothers records are all incontestable Baby Boomer victories, trophies that are constantly pulled down off the shelf and flaunted in the faces of despairing Gen Xers, who can never hope to attain such Olympian heights of pan-terrestrial idealism and multicultural flippancy.

But when it comes to accepting responsibility for everything that has gone wrong in American society during their long cultural suzerainty, Baby Boomers are nowhere to be found. They know that the crack epidemic is a direct outgrowth of enlightened sixties attitudes toward recreational drugs, but they prefer to blame it on a pathologically self-destructive underclass. They know that they personally destroyed Broadway by failing to identify *Phantom* and *Evita* as the cultural equivalent of Adolf Hitler's reindustrialization of the Ruhr Valley, but they like to pretend that well-heeled lepers from Japan and Brazil are responsible for Andrew Lloyd Webber's baleful career. Faux Democrat Baby Boomers know that it is impossible to believe in equal opportunity and still send your children to private schools, but send them they do. Baby Boomers know that they are responsible for Billy Joel, guitar masses, disco, Chevy Chase, a cookie-cutter Fisherman's Wharf in every coastal city, personal wedding vows, school busing, Robin Williams, Anson Williams, Paul Williams, Dennis Rodman, Chris Berman, ABBA, John Denver, Kenny G, John Tesh, Jessica Hahn, Huey Lewis & the News, *Les Miz*, the Gap and Michael Flatley. But when the check for all this carnage arrives, they suddenly go absent without leave. A classic example: demanding their parents admit that Richard Nixon was Beelzebub, but adamantly refusing to admit that Jimmy Carter was Bozo.

An absolute inability to accept the ordinary. One of the most inane Boomer brainchildren is the concept of the Everyday Epiphany, the cosmic koan, the Richter scale emotional event that could happen anytime, anywhere. The result: The ordinary has been rendered extraordinary and the extraordinary rendered prosaic. In olden days— say, 1963—the average person lived in a world where Bar Mitzvahs and First Holy Communions and debutante parties and weddings and funerals were enormously important events fraught with significance that spoke volumes about the human condition. But if you went to see a baseball game, you understood that you were only going to a baseball game. If you took your son out to the ballpark, you were not doing it because you felt that it was an essential rite of passage, a sacred bonding experience that fused your progeny's atman with the abiding spirit of Ruth and DiMaggio and Gehrig and Koufax, phantoms who still patrolled the sacred groves of the green cathedrals. Nor did you suggest that your child was now privy to some shrouded mystery of Ken Burnsian provenance, requiring that one perform the secret Bob Costas handshake in the dark caverns of Ultima Garagiola in order to gain access to the Temple of Lupica in the Forgotten City of Cleveland Alexander. You were simply taking your kid to see the Astros. It was not that big a deal.

Because Baby Boomers are obsessed with living in the moment, they insist that every experience be a watershed, every meal extraordinary, every friendship epochal, every concert superb, every sunset meta-celestial. Life isn't like that. Most meals are okay. Most friendships work until they don't work. Most concerts are decent. Sunsets are sunsets. By turning spectacularly humdrum occurrences into formal rites, Baby Boomers have transmuted even the most banal activities into "events" requiring reflection, planning, research, underwriting and staggering masses of data. This has essentially ruined everything for everybody because nothing can ever again be exactly what it was in the first place: something whose very charm is a direct result of its being accessible, near at hand, *ordinary*.

Tasteful self-absorption as a way of life. Baby Boomers honestly believe that self-indulgence is okay if it is herbal, organic and all-natural, and that greed is acceptable if it includes a cognate self-actualizing component. In fact, greed is only okay if it is naked and predatory. Camouflaged greed can only lead to bad things like moderate Republicanism.

La vita é mia. The typical Baby Boomer has an unshakable faith in the personality-transforming powers of summer vacations. *"I went to Italy, I was exposed to a simpler, more innocent lifestyle, it changed my worldview."* Get real, bwana. You went to a hapless second-and-a-half-world country, you were treated royally by a bunch of people who hate your guts but who desperately need the cash, and then you came back and bored everyone stiff with the details and the hellish slide show: *Cinema Paradiso di Chuck e Becky Milsap*. If your vacation was such an emotional watershed, how come you're still the same schmuck you were before you left? There's nothing wrong with believing that your life is more exciting than other people's. But we don't need to see the photos, and if you insist on e-mailing them, we will just have to hit the "delete unread" button. In the end, it may be true that your entire life is a movie. But it is a home movie. Not even your children would volunteer to watch it.

Retroactive political correctness. When the new one-hundred-dollar bills were introduced in 1996, the beaver fur around Benjamin Franklin's neck had been removed, because Baby Boomers deem the use of animal pelts as clothing depraved and immoral. This was a classic Baby Boomer stealth operation: Let us impose our own values on hopelessly misguided historical figures, administering a retroactive woodshedding to one of the greatest men this country ever produced. By stripping Franklin of his fur collar (North America was actually built on the fur trade), the Treasury Department had fulfilled several criteria of the classic Baby Boomer confrontation. First, as touched up previously: Unlike Davy Crockett, Nathan Hale, John Brown, Martin Luther King, Daniel Boone, Susan B. Anthony or, for that matter, Benjamin Franklin, who went up against some pretty tough customers, Baby Boomers love to pick a fight they can't possibly lose, because their adversary is weak, outnumbered, old, decrepit, poor or dead. Second, they love to impose their values where they are least likely to have any effect. Third, they are determined to do everything in their power to ensure that the past becomes as vapid and stifling and predictable and uninteresting as the present.

Suffering by association. A dysfunctional penchant for vicarious participation in other peoples' tragedies, this might be best described as *virtual misfortune hunting*. Unlike their parents, who actually lived through the Great Depression and in many cases fought in World War II, Boomers tend to claim as their touchstone experiences events that happened somewhere else to someone else. My Lai. Woodstock. Altamont. The Tet Offensive.

Baby Boomers love to act as if the bullets James Earl Ray used on Martin Luther King also winged them. We should be so lucky. Get a few Campari spritzers into a Baby Boomer and he'll tell you that when Malcolm X or Janis Joplin or Jim Morrison or Jimi Hendrix or even that goofy-looking harmonica player from Canned Heat died, a part of him died with them. And then there is the classic Boomer parlor trick of revealing where they were when JFK died. "I can still remember, like it was only yesterday," they love to say. *Yeah, well, so can Caroline.* Again and again, Baby Boomers trot out the same waterlogged mythology, using tragedies that occurred when they were young as a smoke screen for their crassness in middle age. "After Bobby Kennedy died, I felt that the American Dream had died with him," they tell you. "That's why I got into derivatives."

Few things are more unnerving than the Boomer habit of annexing another person's suffering and then adorning it with some ludicrous personal iconography. For example, patronizing restaurants with names like Paris Commune, perhaps hoping that the valor of seventeen thousand Frenchmen massacred in 1871 will rub off on them as they scarf down the *andouilletes* with lobster, leeks and white truffle oil. This is why no Boomer concert is complete without a song about Victor Jara or the massacre in Tiananmen Square or *las abuelitas* (the little grandmothers) who gather in the central plaza of Buenos Aires every Sunday to protest the murder of their grandchildren. Attention, shoppers: David Crosby and Richard Shindell songs are not going to bring back the *desaparecidos*. And singing about heroes is not heroic.

Sometimes it gets more personal. A friend once wrote me a letter anguishing over his wife's reluctant decision to terminate an unwanted pregnancy. For years and years afterward, my friend said, he continued to be haunted by the memory.

"My wife's abortion was my Vietnam," he wrote, the outline of his tears still visible on the stationery.

"Your wife's abortion was your wife's abortion," I wrote back. "Leave Vietnam out of it."

Rock criticism. Before Baby Boomers came along, the *New York Times* never published sentences like this: "That devilish side that leads him [Sting] to play with his musical sources and not just absorb them and to write from the perspective of a man who might be as corrupt as he is enlightened is the source of Sting's integrity." It is impossible to see how prose like this improves the human condition.

The concept of selective virtue. In olden days, if you were going to walk around like you were better than everybody else, you actually had to *be* better than everyone else. And you had to be better than everyone else all the time. Virtue was not some kind of part-time job you could punch out of at the end of the afternoon. If you were going to be a saint or a holy man or an alms giver or a Little Sister of the Poor, you couldn't practice sexual abstinence and bathe lepers and succor the lame and honor the Lord thy God half the time and spend the rest of the time sleeping with the farm animals. Virtue was an all-or-nothing proposition; either you were on the bus or you were off.

Boomers demolished this system by introducing such weird moral hybrids as vegetarians who smoke, pacifists who sell drugs and Buddhists who can get you in on that e-tailing IPO at 7½. These people have adopted the attitude not so much that half a loaf is better than none, but that half a loaf is better than you. This is definitely not what Saint Francis had in mind.

Hypocrisy as a manageable lifestyle. Boomer culture derives from a pathological need to have everything and its exact opposite. I want to dress like I'm poor but actually be rich. I want to dodge the draft but also vote for John McCain. I want to make movies that ridicule people who are lame, tired, out of date and hapless, but still get to be Danny Aykroyd. I want to spend the whole of my youth reading books deploring the moral bankruptcy of my parents' generation, then, when I am in a position to inherit their life's savings, ostentatiously cover the coffee table with stacks of kiss-ass *My Pop the War Hero*–type memoirs praising their extraordinary valor.

Consider the behavior of several Boomer prototypes. Bill Clinton wants to be the moral leader of the Free World. But he also wants to get a little trim on the side. Bill Clinton wants to help the poor. But he also wants to eliminate welfare. Bill Clinton strongly supports public education. But he also wants to send his daughter to private school. He fits neatly into the grand tradition of the Great American Phony.

Other Boomers follow the same game plan. Madonna hawks her line of Catholic showgirl's iconographic accessories in her churlishly sacrilegious videos, then names her child Lourdes and wonders if the pope might baptize her. Ben & Jerry make a fortune thumbing their nose at "evil" giant corporations and then sell their countercultural ice cream company to an "evil" giant corporation. Dennis Miller, the very definition of the maverick shill, poses as the outsider who rants against straight, uptight, Republican America and then signs on as an announcer on *Monday Night Football*. Geraldo Rivera writes a sordid autobiography entitled *Exposing Myself,* then wants to replace Tom Brokaw as one of the "wise men" who sit in judgment in NBC's inner sanctum. The entire generation has driven itself insane by failing to realize that if you want your cake, you simply must stop eating it.

Self-reinvention ad nauseam. Self-reinvention, which derives from the Christian notion that any penitent sinner is capable of achieving redemption, means that all people are capable of repackaging themselves. But the Good Book only intended for people to reinvent themselves once per lifetime, not twenty-five. Cher has been reinventing herself since she was eighteen. Bob Dylan has been doing it since he was twenty-five. Sting reinvents himself every fourth album track. Madonna reinvents herself as a singer every time the public de-invents her as an actress. The driving force behind self-reinvention is the unflagging belief that nothing one does ever goes on one's permanent record. Baby Boomers learned from Jerry Rubin and Jerry Brown and Jerry Springer that the secret to success is to simply keep the target moving. And moving. And moving.

The incessant invocation of sixties mythology. Let's get one thing clear about the sixties: It was not a simpler, more innocent time. It was a nightmare. Everyone hated one another. Everyone was shooting at one another. Civil war was in the air. The food was abysmal. There were race riots in almost every major city. Drugs ravaged the underclass. People got lynched. The only good things about the sixties were the music and the fact that it wasn't the seventies. But even rock 'n' roll was problematic, since people were always getting stuck with worthless tickets because Jim had been arrested for whipping out his cock or Janis had overdosed or Jimi had gagged on his own vomit. I wouldn't live through the sixties again if you paid me. Which is pretty amazing, because Baby Boomers will do just about anything if you pay them.

Premature nostalgia. Baby Boomers were the first generation to become nostalgic for the past before the past had officially arrived. Think of it: classic rock, Beatlemania, CBS golden oldies, all of which are seventies concoctions, fast on the heels of . . . the seventies. All of which are now fixtures in this era of permanent nostalgia. Previous generations had hearkened back to earlier times, but they at least allowed a decent interval to pass before initiating the hearkening. By contrast, twenty-three-year-old Baby Boomers started pining for the good old days when they were only twenty-one. Most of them stopped buying new records during their senior year of college. Don't believe me? Talk to anyone who's ever tried selling them a record. Other than *Graceland*.

Refusal to leave the stage they weren't even on in the first place. Ordinary Baby Boomers love to form old-fogey weekend-warrior bands so they can butcher songs by AC/DC and Aerosmith, and re-butcher songs by Foghat and Deep Purple. Often they bring their kids. No matter how toxic Dorian and Madison are, they probably don't deserve this. And then there are the Celebrity Old Fart Bands like John McEnroe's various groups and Stephen King's Rock Bottom Remainders. It's bad enough that these guys can't take a hint. But then they have to go out and invent new hints not to take.

Self-congratulatory obviousness. Almost without exception, Baby Boomers read the same books, eat the same food, raise the same kids and have the same values as their peers, but insist that they have developed their own intensely personal navel-gazing style. Every Baby Boomer acts like he was the first person to think up some incredible banality (white kids love hip-hop, the French are rude, Republicans seem to be very interested in the bond market), even though they all get their opinions from the same magazines and Web sites. (The habit of introducing these banalities into a conversation in an imperious, semi-oracular fashion is sometimes referred to as "delivering the Full Quindlen.") Just once it would be nice to meet a Baby Boomer who doesn't fall hook, line and sinker for the Legion of Just-Add-Water pundits (Anthony Lewis, Ellen Goodman, Molly Ivins, Bill Moyers). Just once it would be nice to meet a Baby Boomer who actually dislikes the work of Stephen Hawking, Merchant Ivory, Harry Connick, Jr., Maya Angelou. It would be like meeting a Scotsman who announces, "This round's on me."

Preemptive destruction of the future. Though this is the last major accusation I will level at my generation, it is by no means the least serious. Basically, Baby Boomers sabotaged the future by making it a place filled with garbage excavated from the past. If something in the past is unquestionably stupid or unnecessary, you can bet that Baby Boomers will revive it in some jejune, post-ironic way, because Baby Boomers are never really comfortable with anything until it has been dead, buried, exhumed and repackaged. Baby Boomers rarely trust their first impression of things; they usually wait until their eighth impression before finally making up their minds.

VH-1's wildly successful *Behind the Music* is a sterling example of this phenomenon. I will be the first to admit that I enjoy watching a weekly show where I find out that the guys from bands like Whitesnake or Kiss or Grand Funk Railroad wasted all their money on limos or women or drugs or all of the above and are now pasting up billboards or doing time or dead. But I hate it when they announce that they're going back into the studio, that they're planning a limited tour, that *they're coming back*. To me, the whole appeal of the show is to be reminded how terrific the present is precisely because none of these people are in it. Often I think of how great this society would be if all of the truly horrible people went away and stayed away instead of constantly climbing out of the grave. Think of it. No Geraldo. No Mike Milken. No Sylvester Stallone. Conceivably, no Kathie Lee.

This is one thing you really have to give Cat Stevens credit for. Once he went away, he stayed away. He left his career behind. True, he did poke his head out of the foxhole recently, but basically the rest of us haven't heard a peep out of him for twenty years. Twenty years isn't a lifetime, but I'll take it. If only every other Baby Boomer would follow Cat's inspiring example, this place would be Paradise.

2

High Misdemeanors

- -

A man is sitting on a park bench seven thousand feet above sea level, directly across from the snowcapped peaks of the Olympic Mountains. The glacier-speckled summits are spectacularly vivid on this clear July afternoon, silhouetted against a Maxfield Parrish sky as blue as Merryweather's gown in *Sleeping Beauty*. But the man, who we have reason to believe is named Mel, is oblivious to all this useless beauty; inexplicably, he has turned his back on the natural wonders he would almost certainly give his life to defend from nefarious logging companies or perfidious developers. Instead, he is gabbing in an irksome nasal pitch.

Most of the other people in the rest area are chatting in subdued tones, if they are talking at all, as they presumably subscribe to the theory that snowcapped mountains on a 90-degree day beggar speech. But our subject is thundering away full-throttle, sharing his thoughts with the plain, somewhat harried-looking woman sitting directly across from him. By design or happenstance, he is also sharing his thoughts with everyone else within a fifty-yard area. From the look on the woman's face, it is apparent that this is not the first time her companion has held forth in informal public forums on subjects such as this, nor will it be the last. He is a man of strong opinions; he has crafted these opinions over a lifetime of sober reflection; and the opinions that he holds are ones he is anxious to share with all and sundry.

The subject of today's peroration is carbonation.

The speaker is fiftyish, chunky, attired in that eclectic yet oddly troubling uniform that has become the unofficial garb of the environmental paramilitaries who haunt the wide open spaces of this great nation. On his head, inevitably, is perched one of those ill-advised olive-green camouflage sun hats that suggest that the owner is either:

(1) a veteran of a pointless yet tragic foreign war waged in some tropical paradise transmogrified into a living hell;

(2) Woody Allen.

Stylistic incongruities abound as our eyes wander down the subject's legs. His pudgy tootsies have been jammed into gray ankle socks protruding from moss-colored hiking boots, effecting a look that was extremely popular with portly BMW middle-managers vacationing in the Pays Basque area of southwest France in the mid-to-late 1970s, until outraged veterans of the French resistance submitted a formal protest to the German government. Moving up to the trunk, we find military shorts on pacifist thighs and antiwar buttocks, but where there should be a T-shirt emblazoned with some confrontational but ultimately inoffensive message asserting something flamboyantly cheeky (QUESTION REALITY, VISUALIZE WHIRLED PEAS), we find instead a well-worn, button-down shirt of a puzzling lavender hue.

In toto, it is a richly variegated outfit imbued with a quasi-military theme indicating that the wearer is a serious individual, a man of substance. Yet at the same time, the incongruous, gently subversive, delicately ironic lavender shirt certifies that this is a rebel, a loner, a man who goes his own way, a postmodern Shane: a maverick, if you will. Due to follic reverses sustained a quarter-century earlier, he does not have, nor could his head ever sustain, a credible ponytail. But one suspects that had he been dealt a better tonsorial hand, he would now be sporting a full Chaya Brasserie–circa 1988–surly waitstaff–Genghis Khan–piglet's tail from his gaping bald spot like a minotaur's entrails. Well, entrail.

Much thought has gone into this postmodern getup, but not nearly as much as has gone into the subject of carbonation.

"I never drink Coca-Cola on a hot day," he apprises his companion in his booming yet whiny voice. "There's too much sugar in it; it doesn't quench your thirst. And all that carbonation isn't good for you. On a hot day you should drink water. It's much more thirst-quenching. And it doesn't have carbonation. I don't like all that fizz. That's why I only drink flat water, not sparkling water. I never drink sparkling water on hot days like this."

Since he possesses a bullhorn for a voice, people as far away as Yellowknife have a pretty clear idea by now of where he stands on the subject of summer refreshment, carbonation, beverages in general. Not to mention where he figures in the generational scheme of things. For this brief tableau provides a perfect prism through which can be viewed several of the most objectionable Baby Boomer characteristics. A failure to come to terms with deeply unsatisfactory hair. Confusing clothing suggesting that the person has seen subtropical action, perhaps during the invasion of Sierra Leone, Sierra Madre, Sierra Morena or Sierra Club. The tragic miscegenation of Casual Friday, Earth Day, Manic Monday and Weekend Warrior, unwisely mixing conventional workplace attire with authentic military and hiking gear. The profoundly foolish hat. But most important of all, the *canned riff*.

Perhaps nothing distinguishes Baby Boomers from their parents more than the pathological need to share the canned riff with everyone in the immediate vicinity. It is a carefully rehearsed, artisanally crafted spiel that delineates *who I am and how I got here, what I stand for and what I deplore*. Sometimes it involves a particular foodstuff, and why one does not eat it. Sometimes it concerns textures ("I use chopsticks because I love the feel of wood on my tongue"). Sometimes it embraces politics ("I could never vote for a Republican after Reagan laid that wreath at Bitburg"). And sometimes it addresses carbonation ("It's fizzy. It's gassy. It doesn't quench your thirst").

What makes the canned riff so special is that it is a menace of relatively recent provenance. The evil stepchild of Jack Kerouac, Lenny Bruce, Mort Sahl and Abbie Hoffman, the canned riff as a mass phenomenon is a verbal conceit that did not exist before the 1960s. In this sense, the riff is the Baby Boomer equivalent of the cotton gin or the wheel. It is what Boomers have bequeathed to the world, their all-consuming desire to share lovingly manicured, totally unsolicited opinions with complete strangers on subjects that nobody else could possibly care about.

Baby Boomers, from early childhood, were raised to believe not only that their opinions mattered but that they should have a lot of them, and that they should prepare them on all topics. The opinions are part and parcel of a rehearsed eccentricity that ostensibly distinguishes the Garrulous Ass (*Pontificator Maximus*) from the teeming masses. In this case, what our subject is really saying is: Coke may be okay for 1.7 billion other people, but not for Melvin, Lion of the Republic.

I mention the Garrulous Ass not only because he is instantly recognizable, but because his entire carriage and delivery so typify his generation. This type of individual is no longer an anomaly in this society. In many ways, he has become an almost archetypal figure, a fixture of contemporary American folklore as ubiquitous and recognizable as the mooch, the dude, the *putz*, the loser, the tightwad, the greenhorn, the mensch, the head case, the flunky and the stud.

Mel is not a monster. He is not a skinhead. He is not a biker. He is not a neo-Nazi. He is not a gangsta. He is not spewing phlegm on passing children. He has no open sores. Yet in his own way he is every bit as offensive as all these other social misfits. Because unlike them, he is ubiquitous. He is the classic pain-in-the-ass Boomer who has to share his opinions with everybody about everything, and he has to do it all the time. ("I notice that T-shirt you're wearing today. I like it" is a typical unsolicited opinion. "I love *Fortune* magazine. It speaks to me" is another.) The Garrulous Ass can never process the information that no one really cares about his soft-drink philosophy, or how he arrived at it. Were he Napoleon Bonaparte, Cosimo de' Medici, the Landgrave of Smyrna or the thirteenth Laird of Gight, we might be interested in listening to his carbonatory thoughts for about fifteen seconds. He is not. He is a wanker. He is a dink. He is a motormouth. He is the latest in a long line of jack-offs who probably went to Bard.

To understand Mel and his ilk it is necessary to address the concept of the Personal-Size Cosmos. *L'univers, c'est moi* is the philosophy of the fiftyish Baby Boomer mounted on his $2,500 Lance Armstrong model thirty-nine-speeder, who will not slow down while careening across the Golden Gate Bridge, putting small children's lives at risk, because he is racing against his personal best time. He has abundant company. The investment banker on the Metroliner driving everyone else to distraction with his cellphone blather about contextualizing the New Paradigm. The suburban oaf with the blast-furnace leaf blower. The crass simpleton with the state-of-the-art car alarm. In all of these instances, the message is the same: "My rights end where yours begin. You have no rights. Therefore, my rights extend forever."

A common complaint registered against Baby Boomers by their parents is that they never touch each other when they dance. There is a reason for this. Baby Boomers are dancing with themselves. They have been dancing with themselves since first light of day. Go to any outdoor summer music festival and you are certain to see a score of middle-aged men, several dressed like Merlin, twitching solo in that spastic Druid-Navajo rain dance that became so popular in the late sixties. One would like to believe that they are doing this because their partners are long since dead, but this is rarely the case. Their mates, clad in grungy blue overalls and faded, tie-dyed T-shirts, are merely somewhere else, also dancing by themselves. They've been dancing to the music in their own heads since they were sixteen.

Why should they stop now?

ONE OF THE great myths about Baby Boomers is that they started out as valiant, idealistic youths (the Freedom Riders, Woodstock, Four Dead in Ohio, driving Nixon from office, Jon Voigt in *Midnight Cowboy*), and only over time became total sellouts, hypocrites, cowards. This is not true. From the very beginning, Baby Boomers had one dominant characteristic: They were annoying beyond belief. They were never terribly interested in results; they were merely interested in getting under older people's skin. The 1968 Democratic National Convention is a good example. Baby Boomers wanted to end the war in Vietnam. They also wanted to eliminate racism. And they wanted to advance the cause of feminism. So they descended on the city of Chicago, annoyed the hell out of everybody for a whole week and cost Hubert Humphrey, a perfectly decent man, the presidency. As a result of their megalithic annoyingness, Richard Nixon was elected president. *Oh, now* that's *better.* Unlike earlier, supposedly idealistic, generations who posed a clear threat to the established order, Baby Boomers were never much more than a pain in the ass. Their hair was annoying. Their clothes were annoying. Their diction, hygiene, music, literature, art and core beliefs were all annoying. Then, oddly enough, when they grew up, they moved heaven and earth to erect complex lifestyles dedicated to shielding themselves from anything that struck them as even mildly annoying, like poor people or minorities or immigrants or rap music. Now, there's irony for you.

In the previous chapter we focused on egregious Baby Boomer habits, attitudes, values and innovations for which they deserve to be executed. In this chapter we will turn things down a notch or two and concentrate on transgressions that are not in and of themselves meritorious of decapitation or evisceration, but have certainly made this society a much less pleasant place to live in. As was the case in the previous chapter, I cannot imagine that any serious person will contest these charges.

Bootlegs. Once upon a time, the entertainment industry operated on the assumption that while the public might be willing to listen to one version of Jerry Vale's "Volare," they probably did not want to listen to 2,316. Baby Boomers upset the natural order of things by introducing illegal bootlegs and then popularizing the sale of rarities collections containing "alternate takes" of famous songs. Purists, aficionados and anyone with half a brain recognize "alternate takes" as unusable tracks that got left off the album because somebody screwed up. Now they are considered long-lost buried treasure. The upshot: If you find yourself at the wrong Boomer party, you might have to listen to any one of 235 different versions of "Sugar Magnolia."

And some still insist that this universe is ruled by a merciful God.

Vicarious mythology. Baby Boomers who never saw Hendrix, did drugs, locked or loaded an AK-47 in country or bedded down with a girl named Radiance now all pretend they did. It's like those Civil War reenactment buffs who have drunk so much Wild Turkey they actually think they were at Chickamauga. What could be more revolting than Boomers who spent the Summer of Love working in an armaments factory, yet who now caper around with ponytails and tie-dyed shirts pretending that they were kicking out the jams when they came in the morning to take the power from the people back in the days of rage? In other words, Baby Boomers who were not actually annoying when they were young but who now masquerade as annoying people from way back. This makes it impossible for other generations to tell whether the person is behaving like a jerk because he has always been a jerk or because he has assembled a composite image of how jerks used to behave back in the good old days and is now acting it out for real. Only Baby Boomers are capable of such anachronistic annoyingness.

Once-in-a-lifetime events immortalized on mass-produced T-shirts. The man sitting across from you on the subway is wearing a Greek fisherman's cap and a pastel T-shirt emblazoned with the message I CROSSED THE ARCTIC CIRCLE. Hey, tubby, who hasn't? The dentist who lives down the street from me says he personally knows three people who have climbed Mount Everest. They may even be three mountain-climbing dentists. This sort of modular, prefab exoticism, a staple of Robert James Waller's fiction, is just another excuse for Baby Boomers to tell everyone else how special they are. By this late date, crossing the Arctic Circle on foot or kayak or even in a tandem bicycle marathon is about as noteworthy as owning an original-cast recording of *Starlight Express*.

The ubiquitous subtext. Baby Boomers grew up believing that either the CIA or the FBI—and probably both— killed John Kennedy and Martin Luther King, deposed Salvador Allende, sabotaged the antiwar movement, undermined the McGovern campaign, and basically ran the whole country and, by extension, the entire planet, from a secret subterranean headquarters. They also believed that large corporations were using subliminal advertising to make people buy cars they did not really want or even like. In addition they believed that a mysterious but unquestionably massive cabal of shadowy, low-key WASPs secretly controlled the country, and that their very invisibility was the most damning proof of their all-encompassing power.

Given this high level of paranoia, Boomers ultimately came to believe that everything contained a hidden meaning, an imperceptible undercurrent, a veiled subtext. This engendered such concepts as "coding," the technique by which the forces of all-encroaching darkness used seemingly harmless euphemisms such as "underclass" to convey powerful and often negative thoughts about certain ethnic or demographic groups.

Here is an example: I was once a guest on an inconsequential cable TV program where the subject was personal responsibility. I had just written a tongue-in-cheek op-ed piece in the *Washington Post* congratulating Jeffrey Dahmer for apologizing for his cannibalism and accepting full responsibility for his acts; I volunteered that this was the first time in living memory that anyone in America had taken responsibility for his actions and that I looked forward to more apologies of this sort. A woman who was also a guest on the show said that in her business she had to be very sensitive to specific code words, and suggested that by congratulating Jeffrey Dahmer for his remorse I was secretly launching a coded offensive on the urban poor. The moderator asked me to respond to this. I suggested that the woman was an idiot. The woman took this to be another code word. It was not. By and large, when people use the word "idiot," they are not using it to suggest something else.

That whole Eastern thing. Seriously, folks, if we really believed that life was vague, misty, impenetrable, or that the I Ching, the Bhagavad-Gita or the Tibetan Book of the

Dead were likely to help us out of a tight spot, why the hell did we buy Yahoo at 175?

Totally unacceptable hair. There is a point at which middle-aged men with Art Garfunkelian hair cease to be foolish-looking and actually start frightening the people around them. Personally, I believe that small children should not be subjected to this.

Prefab sarcasm. A few generations ago people were expected to be decent. Now everyone is supposed to be clever. The whole country is infested with constitutionally unamusing people who think they're hilarious. Or worse, sardonic, particularly when in the presence of any real emotion. As soon as someone starts telling a genuinely sad story, Boomers have to rev up rehearsed inanities like "Thanks for sharing" or "I'm there for you" or "I feel your pain," in the hope that this will make them appear raffish and witty and less of a schlemiel than the person being ridiculed. If there was only one preening turd like Dennis Miller in this society, the Republic would be safe. But there are seventy-five million of them.

Ostentatious displays of multicultural sensitivity. Like raving about *The Buena Vista Social Club* sound track, even though the only Latinos you ever hope to meet are the maid and the gardener.

Rehearsed political hysteria. Baby Boomers, drama queens par excellence, like to portray every political spat as the psychological equivalent of the Battle of Stalingrad, using brackish, idiotic terms like *kulturkampf*. The spiel runs like this: If Reagan gets elected, you might as well start polishing your jackboots. Or: If Clinton wins, it's *Chairman Mao's Quotations* for everyone. This rehearsed, knee-jerk neuroticism was adroitly captured in the 2000 Whitney Museum of American Art biennial, where one artist tried to portray New York City mayor Rudy Giuliani as a fascist. If you think Rudy Guiliani is a fascist, what are you going to do when the fascists get here?

Front-running like there's no tomorrow. Baby Boomers love to depict themselves as the champions of the underdog, just because they took the Vietcong and the points back in 1967. In reality, Baby Boomers are the most ferocious front-runners ever. Unlike their dads, who lived and died with the Dodgers, the Cubs, the Phillies, and who would have rather slit their own throats than switch their allegiances, Baby Boomers will never reveal who they're rooting for until one team is at least eight runs ahead. If they really loved the underdog as much as they say they do, then how come you never see guests on the *Tonight* show wearing Milwaukee Brewers caps? Or rooting for Surinam in the Olympics? The truth is, Baby Boomers love athletes who have lunch-pail attitudes but hate people who actually carry lunch pails. And they hate losers. During the 1992 presidential campaign, I went out with a TV crew into Times Square and asked people wearing baseball caps who they were going to vote for in the election. I predicted that if they were wearing caps associated with the defending champion Chicago Bulls, Dallas Cowboys or Toronto Blue Jays, they would be voting for the candidate who was currently ahead in the polls. The survey proved infallible. Determined to be in the winner's circle, no matter what is being contested, Baby Boomers are the kind of people you would have seen walking around the streets of ancient Rome in A.D. 71 wearing SPQR RULES! on their togas, but then confiding that they were secretly rooting for the Jews.

Needlessly complicating everything. You know what I'm talking about. Dueling cooking oils, some derived from cold-pressed taggiasca and Calamata olives. Reams of arcane statistics like "batting average against left-handed pitchers with men on base over the last four games." Penne instead of pasta. Four-hundred-easy-repayment plans. Menus containing entries like "Niman Ranch Applewood Smoked Ham and Fontana Panini," as if anyone knows or cares what the Niman Ranch is. Twenty-one-gear bikes. Talmud-scale liner notes accompanying totally extraneous products like the *Box Tops* boxed set. Not to mention inexplicable products like "greatest hits" records by musicians who never had any hits.

And let's not forget coffee. Fifty different kinds of coffee. Fifty different flavors of coffee. Fifty different ways of growing coffee. Fifty different containers for the coffee, all described in that weird hybrid of Italian, French and Spanish best thought of as Starbucks Esperanto. Plus cappuccino frothers. And thirty-five different kinds of chai tea.

In addition to general fussiness, Baby Boomers are universally known for their astounding preciousness. Saying things like "Ceiling fans make me dizzy." Claiming to suffer from weird allergies, like to plastic. And, because they believe that the quality that is best is the quality that can be perceived by the smallest number of people, never looking for the best fabric or the best cut in an article of clothing, but always for something unimaginably arcane, like the precise manner in which the buttonholes are sewn. Preferably by ambidextrous Uruguayan midgets.

Here's a typical Baby Boomer gambit: purporting to be able to distinguish between the medicinal properties of garlic grown in low-lying fields and garlic grown on the sides of mountains. Which is hardly surprising; during the Firestone tire recall crisis of 2000, the *Wall Street Journal* ran a story about a tire dealer in Ohio who would bring his own little set of glasses to wine-tasting events. That's right: a bon vivant tire dealer.

Finally, Baby Boomers are afflicted by an insane need for Himalayas of micro-data before even the slightest purchasing decision can be made. Several years ago, *Consumer Reports*, the bible of Baby Boomers, actually rated peanut butters. Top-of-the-line shoulder bags that come with wise and winsome explanatory literature and upscale ski-jackets whose laundering instructions are as voluminous as *War and Peace* are bad enough. But peanut butter rankings? What's next? Comparisons of ear swabs? Garbage bag ties?

Needlessly complicating everything and then yammering on about the search for "simplicity." Who but the Baby Boomers could have dreamed up something as idiotic as *Real Simple* magazine? Who else would fill their leisure time with books and magazines and courses about feng shui, yachting, calligraphy, mountain-biking, the joy of soy, tantric sex, out-of-body experiences, three-minute abs, quantum therapy, communicating with dead loved ones, Qi Jong, lower back pain, telepathic communication with animals, Buddhism, woodworking, preparing sushi, realigning one's chakras, Incan pottery, self-hypnosis, chatting with trustworthy angels, Mayan prophesies, vibrational sound healing, nonsurgical face-lifts, mat cutting and municipal bonds, and then act like one more dumb-ass magazine put out by jaded yuppie journalists in New York City could possibly improve their lives? When previous generations had problems organizing their lives, they turned to religion or literature or genies. When Baby Boomers have problems organizing their lives, they turn to Time Warner and AOL. This is not the answer.

Insistence that everyone share the same emotions in the presence of communal misfortune. Though they like to think of themselves as quiet loners who go their own way and march to the beat of a different drummer, Baby Boomers are uncomfortable when anyone deviates from the unwritten law of official sentimentality. One of Bill Clinton's greatest strengths is his ability to open his handy emotions kit and pair an event with the proper response, without any interest whatsoever in whether this would actually improve the situation at hand. *"Bosnians, I feel your pain." "African-Americans, I am there for you." "My Mexican brothers, is* nuestra familia *not on the same page?"* Like Clinton, Baby Boomers don't actually care what other people *do* as long as they *say* the right things, as long as they consult the prescribed stimulus-response chart, select the appropriate sentiment, add water, and then emote. This is a technique they learned from Jean-Jacques Rousseau, who invented the concept of inefficacious sincerity.

Let me close this section by offering an example of this peculiar phenomenon. One afternoon I was visiting a friend who was dying. There were several others in the room, who were dealing with the tragedy in their own different ways. A couple of them were hugging people. A couple of them were aging flower children.

I have nothing against hugging per se, but I never hug strangers, because a hug implies an intimacy that we could not possibly share. Moreover, flower children never let me touch them when they were young and nubile, so why should I hug them now that they are old and fat? Though my body language emphatically stated that I was the non-embraceable type, I could see the most intrepid of the huggers heading directly toward me. Hoping to spare us both the embarrassment of a spurned hug, a rebuff the other people in the room might misinterpret as a lack of emotional depth, I cut her off at the pass by leaving the room.

Standing in the hallway, I heard the woman come up behind me. We were clearly in one of those competitive deathbed scenarios that Baby Boomers love, with each of us expected to divulge how profoundly, irreversibly devastated we would be once the doomed friend was dearly departed. I do not perform well in situations such as this, as I come from a long line of insensitive people, and generally handle tragedy rather well. Or in this case, by her lights, not well.

After an awkward silence, she spoke: "It's a shame that men have so much trouble showing their emotions," she whispered. It was classic Baby Boomer feminism. What she meant was: *"You probably have the same feelings that I do, but you can't possibly show them, because that would necessitate revealing your feminine side, which this hideously repressive society prohibits you from doing."* It was also classic Baby Boomer behavior in that it capitalized on an inappropriate, emotionally devastating moment to launch a skirmish in the ongoing gender wars.

"Actually, I have no trouble showing my emotions," I told her. "These are my emotions. I'm sad that my friend is dying, and that's why I look so sad. If my friend wasn't dying, I would probably be smiling and look a lot happier. I think a lot of men work this way."

"Have a nice life," she replied.

Ditto.

3

The Disclaimer Chapter

I was already about a third of the way through writing this book when I realized that some readers might take issue with my methodology. If my putatively rigorous scientific approach failed to pass muster with readers, I might be forced to rethink some of my arguments, pulp everything I had already written, and start all over again. That would have been what we used to call *an unmitigated disaster* back in the days when everything was everything.

The first matter to be addressed was the precise definition of the term "Baby Boomer." As popular lore has construed it, Baby Boomers are the progeny of a rich, powerful, confident America, emboldened by its stunning victories over fascism and the Great Depression. Sociologists and demographics experts certify the Baby Boom as beginning in 1946, immediately after the Second World War, and extending up to 1962, the year before John F. Kennedy was assassinated, or 1964, the year of the British pop music invasion. The children of privilege, the children of opportunity, Baby Boomers are the first generation of Americans born directly into the lap of luxury.

For a number of reasons, I have never been comfortable with this chronological straitjacket. To my way of thinking, the term "Baby Boomer" describes a mind-set as much as it defines a demographic group. To qualify as a Baby Boomer, a person must have been deeply affected at a relatively early age by a significant number of the following: the Soviet Union's development of the hydrogen bomb, Elvis, Sputnik, the Thunderbird, the Twist, the 1960 Nixon-Kennedy debate, the Bay of Pigs, the Cuban Missile Crisis, Muhammad Ali's defeat of Sonny Liston, JFK's assassination, the Beatles, the civil rights movement, Martin Luther King's assassination, Malcolm X's assassination, Robert F. Kennedy's assassination, assorted other assassinations, the Tet Offensive, the Days of Rage, the Strawberry Statement, LBJ's self-furlough, Muhammad Ali's defeat at the hands of Joe Frazier, Jimi Hendrix's death, Jim Morrison's death, Janis Joplin's death, Duane Allman's death, Woodstock, *Easy Rider, The Graduate, Joe, 2001: A Space Odyssey*, Altamont, Charles Manson, the breakup of the Beatles, the secret invasion of Cambodia, Watergate, Richard Nixon's resignation.

In order to qualify as a Baby Boomer, one must have some direct, formative experience with fallout shelters, air-raid drills, hula hoops, bra-burning, acid, meth, speed, hashish, transcendental meditation, and the words "groovy," "hassle," "pusher" and "guru." One must also have some opinion, however slight or ill-conceived, about Patty Hearst, George Wallace, Jane Fonda, Sandy Duncan, *I Am Curious (Yellow)* and whether or not Morrison actually whipped it out onstage in the county of Dade. If one cannot immediately identify the hidden photographic and lyrical clues pertaining to Paul's death on *Magical Mystery Tour*, one is not a full-fledged Baby Boomer. If one never got totally wrecked listening to *Exile on Main Street* or *The Dark Side of the Moon*, one is not a full-fledged Baby Boomer. If one does not know or care what the phrase "25 or 6 to 4" means, one is definitely not a Baby Boomer.

If you are one of those individuals unlucky enough to have been born on the cusp of this generation, here is a handy test enabling you to determine whether you qualify as a full-fledged Baby Boomer.

1) *Baby Boomers lost their innocence at* (A) Altamont; (B) Da Nang; (C) Provence; (D) Chappaquiddick; (E) Vail.

2) *Duane Allman is to Greg Allman as:* (A) Dave Davies is to Ray Davies; (B) John Fogerty is to Tom Fogerty; (C) Johnny Winter is to Edgar Winter; (D) Alex Van Halen is to Eddie Van Halen.

3) *On August 3, 1962, Lee Harvey Oswald and Sirhan Sirhan are paddling a canoe down the Potomac at 12 miles an hour. Meanwhile, Charles Manson, James Earl Ray and Mark David Chapman*

are hurtling toward them in a motorboat cruising at 75 miles an hour. If the two boats collide just south of the Jefferson Memorial, which Baby Boomer hero will still be assassinated in the next few years: (A) Martin Luther King; (B) Bobby Kennedy; (C) John Lennon; (D) John F. Kennedy.

4) *Rank these four Rolling Stones guitarists in declining order of musical talent:* (A) Keith Richard; (B) Mick Taylor; (C) Brian Jones; (D) Ron Wood.

5) *"Bum trip" is to "guilt trip" as:* (A) "acid test" is to "litmus test"; (B) "trip out" is to "freak out"; (C) "far out" is to "space out"; (D) all of the above.

6) *Identify the correct spelling of Sly and the Family Stone's 1969 hit, "Thank You for Letting Me Be Myself Again":* (A) "Thank Ya fa Lettin Me Be Myzelf Agin"; (B) "Thank You for Letting Me Be Myself Again"; (C) "Thank You (Falettinme Be Mice Elf Agin)"; (D) "Thankyoufalettinmebemyzelf-again."

7) *When schoolchildren put their heads under their desks in 1957–1963, they were preparing for* (A) an H-bomb attack by the godless Soviets; (B) an A-bomb attack by the Red Chinese; (C) a *Fail-Safe* type nuclear attack by the United States Air Force to compensate for the inadvertent destruction of Moscow by American ICBMs; (D) all of the above.

8) *Identify the band that is not an outright clone of the group whose name follows it:* (A) Led Zeppelin and Jeff Beck's Truth; (B) the Monkees and the Beatles; (C) America and the Eagles; (D) Aerosmith and the Rolling Stones.

9) *When young women publicly burned their bras back in the late sixties, the average bra size was* (A) 32A; (B) 34C; (C) 36B; (D) 42D.

10) *Match the following Jims with their cause of death:*

Jim Morrison	Airplane Crash
Jimi Hendrix	Booze and drugs
Jim Croce	Probably just drugs

Essay question: *Based on your knowledge of their respective personalities, discuss whether John Lennon would have allowed Paul McCartney to include "Silly Love Songs" on a mid-seventies Beatles' album had the band not broken up in 1970.*

Bonus question: *For additional credit, discuss whether George Harrison was the least intelligent Beatle.*

For answers, consult end of chapter.

Given these parameters, it is clear that the entry point for inclusion in the Baby Boomer generation must be pushed back from 1946 to 1943, and that the cutoff point must be moved back from 1964 or 1962 to 1960. Although the Second World War did not officially end until 1945, the Allies knew that the Japanese were on a slippery slope after the Battle of Midway in 1942 and that the Germans were kaput after the surrender at Stalingrad in 1943. Americans thereupon started having babies in prodigious numbers in preemptive celebration of their inevitable victory. This may very well explain why Baby Boomers are the most confident generation in American history: They were the goodies that spilled out of the piñata at the party America held for itself two years *before* the Germans and the Japanese actually surrendered.

In truth I have another reason for pushing back the on-sale date to 1943. Randy Newman, one of the few famous Baby Boomers who is not a thoroughly revolting human being, was born in 1943. I need him in this book. Conversely, Geraldo Rivera, the quintessence of Baby Boomer moral corruption, was also born in 1943. I definitely need him in this book. I need him in all my books. If I don't get to make a lot of jokes about Geraldo Rivera in my books, I can't see the point in being a writer. I'm certainly not doing this for the money.

IN ASSIGNING A number of general characteristics to Baby Boomers (epic self-absorption, staggering greed, a fiendish obsession with staying young, generally dreadful hair), armchair sociologists might object: Am I not perhaps casting too wide a net? In painting, and indeed tarring, an entire generation with such a wide brush, is it not possible that I have overlooked substantial subgroups in my generation who do not fit the general description of Baby Boomers as I define the term? What about African-American Baby Boomers? Hispanic Baby Boomers? Baby Boomers of color in general? White-trash Baby Boomers? Baby Boomers who voted for Nixon? Baby Boomers who voted for Wallace? In failing to address these statistically relevant subsets, am I not hoisting an entire generation on somebody else's petard, casually indicting perfectly innocent, upstanding forty- and fiftysomethings who have never once thrown a hissy fit just because the gourmet store has run out of zebra tomatoes, never once feigned loss of sleep over the fate of the rain forest, never owned or even dreamed of owning a DVD version of one of those early Eric Rohmer films?

The answer is a carefully qualified "yes." To which I riposte: So what? For better or worse, when employing the term "Baby Boomer," I am basically talking about that stupendously large, spectacularly visible group of people who were born between 1943 and 1960, who came of age in the late sixties and early seventies, who are generally depicted as having been incredibly idealistic in their youths before becoming the navel-gazing twerps that they are now, who were in some way young enough to be scarred by Nixon, but too old to be scarred by Carter. These are the people who participated in the great social upheaval of the 1960s—banishing racism, experimenting with drugs, protesting the war, dabbling in carpentry, pottery and Hopi basket-weaving—before going to work for Morgan Stanley. If you saw the NBC series *The Sixties*, you know the people I'm talking about. Not all Baby Boomers fit this description. Yet, when we speak of Boomers, this is the mental scenery that naturally comes to mind. I cannot help this. Long before Baby Boomers composed a generation, they first embodied a state of mind. Contemporaries who were in a different state of mind will simply have to grin and bear it.

Some observers may protest that what I am really describing here are yuppies, a particularly sinister, but somewhat younger, subset of Baby Boomers. There is a measure of truth to this criticism; the most repugnant Baby Boomers do tend to be the late-blooming yuppies who missed out on most of the upheaval of the sixties, who slid effortlessly from the depravity of the seventies into the naked avarice of the eighties, and who are generally described as "scum." Once again, I view this objection as inconsequential. I am willing to concede that not all Boomers are yuppies, just as I am willing to concede that not all yuppies are Boomers. But there is enough of an overlap between the two groups to make life completely miserable for everyone else in this society for at least another thirty years. And that is what concerns us here, not Jesuitical fiddle-faddle about micro-demographic nuances.

I hope this clarification has been helpful.

IS SUCH A high-handed, unscientific approach fair to downscale Baby Boomers, minority Baby Boomers, redneck Baby Boomers, or right-wing Baby Boomers like Rush Limbaugh? Probably not. But that is their fault for being generationally anomalous. Look at it this way: There are probably French people who aren't a huge pain in the ass, Scottish people who aren't taciturn and cheap, camera-wielding Japanese tourists who don't prowl the Louvre stalking the *Mona Lisa*. But when we use the words "French" or "Scottish" or "Japanese tourist," the ready-at-hand images of the surly frog, the tight-ass Highlander and the irksome Japanese are the ones that get evoked. These may be stereotypes, but they are sufficiently widespread and sufficiently rooted in fact to be in some sense *true*. They are group snapshots. And they are snapshots that any police lab would be happy to work with. They may not be perfectly accurate, but they are definitely in the ballpark. If there is a Japanese tourist in the Louvre who isn't ready to knock over eighteen epileptic senior citizens just to get three inches closer to the *Mona Lisa*, I certainly haven't met him.

Here is some more ammunition in support of my thesis. While it is true that Baby Boomers may diverge in their biographical, socioeconomic and philosophical particulars, it is equally true that all Baby Boomers share certain *general* characteristics that render their generation uniquely toxic. Not every Baby Boomer has a baby named Jackson and a baby monitor in his room to make sure that he is listening to Mozart. Not every Baby Boomer dropped acid. Not every Boomer opposed the bombing of Cambodia, Hanoi, that row home in West Philadelphia.

But every Baby Boomer is pathologically self-absorbed. Every Baby Boomer adamantly refuses to grow up. Every Baby Boomer has conflicted feelings about his own parents' generation, but is absolutely implacable in his hatred of Gen X. Moreover, every Baby Boomer, given the motive, opportunity, financing and appropriate recreational drugs would name his son Jackson and put a baby monitor in his room. Finally, as previously noted, all Baby Boomers have unresolved hair issues.

Conservatives invariably get their hackles up whenever writers describe Baby Boomers this way. They'll talk you blue in the face about how few young people actually opposed the Vietnam War, how the turn-on, tune-in, drop-out Baby Boomers who came to symbolize their generation were always a minority. A large minority, but a minority all the same. Okay, a very large minority, but a minority all the same. All right, a stupefyingly large minority, but a minority all the same. These conservatives—and the occasional libertarian—will produce colorful charts and graphs and statistics to prove this point. They have convinced themselves that their argument is watertight, their position unassailable. Then they get all hot and bothered because no one pays any attention to them.

These petulant conservatives—and that occasional libertarian—steadfastly refuse to accept one of the most honored anthropological principles of the modern age: Where perception is more powerful than reality, reality must give way to perception. When the Mongols raped and plundered their way across Europe in the thirteenth century, they were never able to field an especially large army, as they were thousands of miles from home and the Mongol race was never very numerous. Yet to the civilizations they ravaged, it seemed as if they were everywhere, and it seemed as if there were an awful lot of them. Between 1218 and 1260, you couldn't set foot outside your house between Peking and Prague without having a Mongol horde sweep past and lop your ears off while flaying your grandparents and eating your dog, all without dismounting. By moving quickly, traveling in large packs and placing important people in highly visible positions of authority, the Mongols created a daunting illusion of ubiquity and numerical superiority.

The same situation prevails with Baby Boomers. While it may be true that tie-dyed, hemp-toking countercultural hipsters were never an absolute majority of Boomers, it certainly seemed like it at the time. They were always hamming it up on television. They were always showing off at the sit-ins. They were always burning their bras. They were always scoring reefer. They always knew when the heat was about to come down. They were always going off to live in the shaman's teepee to study Aramaic with a bisexual potter named Coyote. Then, later in life, they were always the ones with the cell phone in the Jeep Grand Cherokee listening to "Will I See You in Heaven?" while going to pick up Jared and Gillian at the soccer match. If these people were not in fact everywhere, they certainly created a hell of a good impression at the time.

I am not denying that among the Baby Boomer generation can be found millions of explicitly hopeless people who were put on this earth to buy John Tesh records and raise their children to work in gas stations, people who have never heard of Herman Hesse and Khalil Gibran and Ravi Shankar, just as there are probably one or two Baby Boomers who play the accordion. But they are not part of our story here. They are mythologically irrelevant, archetypally extraneous. In France during the Revolution of 1789 there were millions of peasants who opposed the actions of Danton and Robespierre, in part because of their ruthless assault on the Church. Nevertheless, the general impression we have taken away from reading about this era is one of millions of bloodthirsty sansculottes led by Madame LaFarge marching on the Bastille, freeing the Man in the Iron Mask, the Marquis de Sade and Charles Darnay's father-in-law, and then chopping off Marie Antoinette's head after she made that dumb wisecrack about the widespread availability of brioche. The little bitch.

During the American Revolution, one-third of the colonists supported the insurrection, one-third were loyal to the Crown, and one-third didn't give a damn one way or the other. But when we conjure up images of the American

Revolution, we visualize George Washington and Paul Revere and Ethan Allen and the rest of those Yankee Doodle Dandies, not all those scabrous loyalists, and certainly not those millions of fence-sitters.

This is the point I wish to drive home here. When I speak of Baby Boomers, I am speaking of the Platonic, archetypal Baby Boomer, that person we all have in our head, or, in my case, in our body. "I can't explain pornography," a famous Supreme Court justice once said, "but I know it when I see it." I feel the same way about Baby Boomers. I can't describe them in the abstract, but I know one when I see one. Sierra Club T-shirt. New Balance running shoes. Overpriced shoulder bag with thirteen pockets. Grand Cherokee, Range Rover, Siena or Explorer (before the tire recall). *Rhythm of the Saints* on the CD player. *Snow Falling on Cedars* in the side compartment. Children named Scott and Erika. Still can't believe the Equal Rights Amendment didn't pass. Anguishes over gun control. Genuinely fears people named Jeb. Never forgave Yoko for the Beatles breakup.

Never, ever will.

Answers to quiz.

1. (A) Altamont. What a bummer that was.

2. (D). Like Duane Allman, Alex Van Halen has a younger brother who married an actress with big hair.

3. (D) John F. Kennedy. Since JFK was actually murdered by the CIA, working in consort with the FBI, the Cosa Nostra, Cuban exiles enraged by JFK's failure to provide air support during the disastrous Bay of Pigs invasion and a cabal of shadowy New Orleans homosexuals, he would still be assassinated

in Dallas on November 22, 1963. As everyone knows, Lee Harvey Oswald was framed.

4. Mick Taylor, Keith Richard, Ron Wood, Brian Jones. Although he founded the Rolling Stones and provided an enormous stylistic influence on sixties fashion, and helped introduce sitars and Eastern weirdness to Western popular music, Brian Jones was actually a terrible guitarist.

5. (D) All of the above. Everything *is* everything.

6. (C). It's the "mice" that always throws people off.

7. (D) All of the above. Things were really, really weird back in the fifties.

8. (C). Since America existed before the Eagles, they could not possibly be a clone of the band.

9. (A) 32A. Women were incredibly flat-chested back in the sixties.

10. Jim Morrison: booze and drugs. Jimi Hendrix: probably just drugs. Jim Croce: airplane crash.

Essay question. John Lennon once threatened to quit the Beatles if Paul insisted on including "Besame Mucho" on the band's first LP. There is no way he would have allowed the Beatles to record "Silly Love Songs." Much less "Ebony and Ivory."

Bonus Question: George was definitely the least intelligent Beatle. Just listen to him talk.

4

Ten Days That
Rocked the World

In seeking to analyze the failed promise of a generation that initially seemed to have so much going for it but ultimately pulled a massive tank job, it is essential to pinpoint the pivotal moments in Baby Boomer history where things went awry. In this chapter we will discuss ten of these moments. I have chosen the number ten because it is a sacred number to Boomers, who honestly believe that all problems can be solved by compiling some form of "Top 10" list, even though in this case the number eight would probably be more accurate. But the number eight lacks numerological elegance, so ten it is.

This list begins with what I view to be the single most important event in the history of the Baby Boomers. But the other nine critical moments are not arranged in any particular order of merit, nor have I arranged them chronologically. I believe that it is up to the reader to determine the ultimate sequence in which these events must be ranked. However, no serious student of the human condition can deny that these events are absolutely essential to an understanding of the Baby Boomer generation.

Exercises of this nature typically proceed from an a priori search for the sine qua non, the ability to identify the pivotal person or event without which history would have been entirely different. Without Jesus Christ, the world would be an even crueler place. Without Marilyn Monroe, the world would be an even duller place. Without Isaac Newton, the world would be an even dumber place. And without Johannes Gutenberg, the world would be an even less erudite place, as there would have been no William Shakespeare, no Leo Tolstoy, no Jane Austen, no David Foster Wallace.

In attempting to isolate the person or event whose existence irretrievably sent Baby Boomers hurtling down the wrong path, resulting in the national crisis we face today, one is presented with numerous strong candidates. Clearly, Richard Nixon must bear a good deal of the blame for Boomer cynicism and moral malleability. Obviously, Timothy Leary must take much of the heat for the drug problems in this country, since it was he who popularized the notion that using hallucinogens on a regular basis would dramatically improve life in these United States. For various reasons, Abbie Hoffman, O. J. Simpson,

Mike Milken and Bill Clinton also merit at least some consideration.

But ultimately, because the Baby Boomers are a rock 'n' roll generation, it is a rock 'n' roll star who must be blamed for the generation's downward spiral. Here again there are many obvious candidates. The saccharine James Taylor. The pallid Paul Simon. The wan Jackson Browne. The tantric Sting. Yet in the end, monstrous though their crimes may be, the person who sparked the whole crisis is not a man. It is a woman. And amazingly, it is not Bette Midler, Pat Benatar, Madonna or Cher.

Number One. April 21, 1971. *Carole King's "Tapestry" is released by Ode Records.* This is a date as ignominious, cataclysmic and final as 1453 (the Turks finally capture Constantinople), 1066 (the Battle of Hastings) or 476 (the fall of the Roman Empire). For it was on this day that Baby Boomers threw in the towel.

Others may remember where they were on March 31, 1968, when Lyndon Baines Johnson announced that he would not seek reelection (actually, I can remember that too. I was at a Jimi Hendrix concert), but I can remember where I was when I first heard "Smackwater Jack." The astonishing popularity of King's mawkish LP (it eventually sold more than 15 million copies and remained on *Billboard*'s Top 40 chart for sixty-eight weeks, including an amazing four months in the No. 1 slot) provided incontrovertible evidence that at heart the Boomers were at least as sappy and corny as their parents.

Tapestry introduced the three themes that would dominate the Baby Boomer mind-set from that point forward:

genteel lameness ("You've Got a Friend"), communal nostalgia for the extremely recent past ("So Far Away," "It's Too Late") and incessant and incorrigible self-repackaging ("Will You Love Me Tomorrow?," a grueling reworking of a hit King had cowritten ten years earlier, now performed at catatonic speed). To these themes social anthropologists might add halfhearted rock feminism of the Helen Reddy/Cher/Carly Simon variety and the rise of the barefoot diva, but I prefer to concentrate on motifs whose importance cannot be challenged nor, for that matter, overstated.

I am certainly not suggesting that *Tapestry* was the first incandescently lame Boomer LP, nor even that it is the most incandescently lame. By the time Carole King released her compendium of syrupy ballads and winsome foot-thumpers in 1971, James Taylor, Crosby, Stills & Nash, Seals & Croft and the various aforementioned people named Simon were already well on their way to eviscerating rock 'n' roll as we knew it, with the term "soft rock" already well on its way to becoming an integral component of the national patois. But *Tapestry* defines a seismic cultural shift, a crack in the zeitgeist fault line, the moment when an entire generation decided to pull up short, pause for reflection, get its bearings and go completely MOR.

When King warbled, "Doesn't anybody stay in one place anymore?" she seemed to be posing a question that everyone under the age of thirty was simultaneously asking themselves. A lot of shit had gone down in the United States in recent years. Innumerable bum trips had been experienced. Too many friends had been wasted on the way. The staggering popularity of the morbidly dull LP marked the moment when an entire generation said, "Doctor my eyes, because although I was in the right place—Selma, Monterey, 'Nam—it must have been the wrong time. Believe me, doc, I have not only seen the needle but the damage done—even though Neil Young will not actually write that song for a couple more years. In conclusion, I am tired. I am stressed. I need to take some time off."

In fact, the Baby Boomers would take the rest of their lives off.

History tells the whole gut-wrenching story. As anyone familiar with late-twentieth-century pop music is well aware, the English Invasion of 1963–64 shattered the cultural hegemony imposed by such frightening homegrown figures as Lesley Gore and the 4 Seasons, and also apprised lovable twerps like the Beach Boys that whatever they'd been doing up until then would no longer do. From the time the Beatles released the primitive "Love Me Do," rock music steadfastly proclaimed itself to be qualitatively different from anything that had gone before. The Stones did not sound like Patti Page; the Doors did not sound like Vic Damone; and the values, tastes and stereophonic equipment of the young people who bought their records bore no resemblance to those of their parents.

It is all well and good for revisionists to rhapsodize about Duke Ellington and Count Basie and the Dorseys, the big guns of the Greatest Generation's era, but in fact all of these big bands had an ambiguous relationship with their supposedly adoring public. Look at it this way: The only big bands that succeeded, and succeeded rather spectacularly, in the popular television arena were Lawrence Welk and his Champagne Music Makers and, to a lesser extent, Guy Lombardo and his Royal Canadians. They were pitiful. The truth is, most of the popular music the Greatest Generation listened to was horrible: Doris Day, Sammy Davis, Jr., Mantovani, sound tracks from idiotic movies, klutzed-up classics by overbearing stooges like Victor Borge, and an endless barrage of moronic novelty songs about using a deck of cards as a Bible, etc. The music was largely dreadful; the music was largely hokey. And whatever else they might be accused of, people growing up in the sixties were not hokey.

Well, not at the start.

Rock music continued on a generally upward, innovative, non-cornball trend until June 1969, when *Tommy* was released. Baby Boomers' enthusiastic embrace of *Tommy* was a tacit admission that ordinary rock music was fundamentally juvenile and needed to set its heights higher. Baby Boomers were now demanding their own Puccini, and Pete Townsend would have to fill the bill. Townsend, in fact, did not fill the bill; that role would fall to Andrew Lloyd Webber. But the ebullient response of young Americans to *Tommy* was the first telltale sign that Baby Boomers possessed a heretofore concealed streak of promethean flatulence in them, presaging a previously unimaginable Billy Joelic/Elton Johnic/Phil Collinsian future.

Cultural historians may challenge this assertion, pointing out that by the time *Tommy* was released, Baby Boomers had already given their seal of approval to any number of pasty-faced, pseudo-Merovingian, neo-faux troubador acts like Donovan, who may have actually believed that he was the reincarnation of Morgan le Fay, and Jethro Tull's Ian Andersen, who probably was. It is undeniable that the Boomers always had a loopy post-Pre-Raphaelite streak in them, and had long been susceptible to Crystal Blue Persuasion in a Gadda-Da-Vida and/or the Court of the Crimson and Clover King, inhaling Incense and Peppermints during Days of Future Passed, which immediately preceded the Nights in White Satin during which the Mellow Yellow Minstrel in the Gallery chanted Songs from the Norwegian Woods or, where the sheet music was not available, Songs from a Garden to a Flower Girl. They were also somewhat partial to tea and oranges that came all the way from China. But that was little more than evanescent Electric Prunes/Strawberry Alarm Clock/Chocolate Watchband/Blues Magoos silliness.

The Who, on the other hand, were a band that people took seriously. They had charisma, attitude, stature. What's more, they were sophisticated. Pete Townsend had once told *Crawdaddy* magazine that Claude Debussy's *La Mer* ranked among his five desert island discs. And John Entwistle could play the French horn. Most important of all, the Who could point to a *body of work* and *an arc to their career* years before people even dreamed about using that sort of terminology. So when the Who started talking about their generation, people listened. *They* weren't going to get fooled again.

After *Tommy*, Baby Boomers became introspective and pretentious. From there it was but one step to sappy and mellow. First came "The Long and Winding Road." Then "Bridge over Troubled Water." Then "Sweet Baby James."

And then, like a laid-back bat out of hell, appeared *Tapestry*, whose very title captures that ambiguous, touchy-feely flight to utterly imperceptible quality—later manifested in a passion for quince paste, apricot *demi-glacé* and Pernigotti cocoa—that would typify the Boomers for the rest of their lives. When Carole King lamented that so many people, many of them so far away, were incapable of staying in one place anymore, she seemed to be saying "It's okay to be nostalgic, even though you're only eighteen. You've seen fire. You've seen rain. So relax. Give in. Go with the flow. Let's put that four dead in O-hi-o thing behind us."

Obviously, every generation dreams of taking early retirement. The Baby Boomers retired in the early seventies. They got all tuckered out from Vietnam and Nixon and the Kennedys and all those race riots and decided that they needed a break. The break never ended. To paraphrase a query made popular during the Watergate hearings, the key question here is "When were you lame and when did you know it?" The answer: April 21, 1971. You can look it up.

Number Two. September 24, 1987. *Ordinary guys start talking about balsamic vinegar.* On September 24, 1987, legend has it, a thirtysomething telemarketing executive named Peter McCabe drove out to the public dump thirty-two miles south of Wheeling, West Virginia, to shoot some rats with his high school buddies. The conversation that night was mostly guy talk—college football, work, tits. As the boys were saddling up to go home, one of them mentioned that he had four tickets to the Morgan State—

72

Marshall game that weekend. "All right!" cheered three of the men.

But Peter said he was not available. Unloading his shotgun, Peter politely explained that he was driving up to Carlisle, Pennsylvania, that Saturday to buy some super-premium balsamic vinegar. Although balsamic vinegar was available at a number of Italian grocery stores in the Greater Wheeling area, the quality was not as high as Peter would have liked, leaving him quite unsatisfied with the crusty sturgeon with rosemary and balsamic vinegar he so loved to prepare on the weekend.

By this time, top-quality balsamic vinegar was all the rage in places like New York and Los Angeles, but it was only just now becoming available in semi-rural back-waters like the outlying suburbs of Wheeling, West Virginia. Peter explained that much as he would like to attend the football game that Saturday, he was very particular about the type of balsamic vinegar he used in his cooking, and could no longer delay making this vital trip.

In Arthur Conan Doyle's classic story "Silver Blaze," Sherlock Holmes finally unravels the mystery of the victimized racehorse by studying the behavior of the household dog. The telltale clue is not that the dog barked but that it did *not* bark, indicating that the intruder was someone it recognized. A similar line of reasoning holds true in the case of Peter McCabe. When Peter told his friends that he could not go to the football game that weekend because he had to go shopping for balsamic vinegar, the amazing thing is not what the other three men did but what they did not do. They did not immediately beat him senseless. This was the first time in American history that an average guy had escaped with his life after begging off a football game because he had to go shopping for the ingredients needed to make his renowned crusty sturgeon. Although basil buffs, cilantro lovers and enthusiasts of balsamic vinegar would continue to figure in a tiny number of mysterious disappearances and apparent suicides in the American hinterland throughout the late 1980s, by the end of the next decade no one in America would give it a second thought if his best friend announced in the middle of a rat-shooting outing that he was driving a few hundred miles that weekend to shop for balsamic vinegar.

Spice buffs and cultural anthropologists may argue that this arguably apocryphal incident is not, in fact, a watershed moment in the history of the Baby Boomers, that the real break with the past would arrive at least five years later, when ordinary men would start asking complete strangers on the subway where they usually purchased the basil they used in their pesto sauce, because frankly they were not terribly thrilled with the efficacy and consistency of the herbs they were buying. Others may single out 1997, the year in which a majority of heterosexual men were actually capable of visually distinguishing between vermicelli and spaghettini without massive amounts of coaching from their wives and girlfriends.

But I disagree. It is my heartfelt belief that once thirty-something Baby Boomer rat hunters felt comfortable enough to discuss their balsamic vinegar–shopping expeditions with their fellow rodent predators, the face of America had changed forever. When young people ask today what Baby Boomers did with all that free time they had after Nixon was run out of office and the civil rights movement trickled away, or, for that matter, what they did with all the time they didn't waste smoking, the answer is easy. They listened to every recording of Vivaldi's *The Four Seasons* they could get their hands on. They read a lot of books about southern France. They attended a lot of past-life regression workshops, moved heaven and earth to empower their inner gods and goddesses, studied ancient Vedic breathing techniques, mastered the art of designing and applying henna-based tattoos, learned how to make candles and massively, though not completely, reduced clutter. And they made one hell of a lot of salads.

Number Three. December 17, 1973. *The Chilean wine boycott.* Shortly after the democratically elected government of Chile was overthrown by Augusto Pinochet's right-wing forces of darkness, left-leaning Americans stopped drinking Chilean wine products and made sure that everyone knew it. In retrospect, giving up Chilean wine was not exactly like giving up toilet paper or sedatives or oral sex; for that matter, it wasn't even like giving up Italian, French or California wine. Since Pinochet's government managed to hang on to power until 1990, and since very few of the people who murdered Allende's followers in the infamous Santiago soccer stadium massacre were ever punished for their atrocities, it's hard to see how the Chilean wine boycott did much good. But the event was important because it provided the first example of the generation-wide hollow gesture, a powerfully resonant action that did nothing for the aggrieved party, but that made protesters feel better about themselves. The Chilean wine boycott never widened into a refusal to eat Japanese tuna or wear sneakers made in Indonesian sweatshops or drink Beaujolais in protest against France's aggressive use of nuclear power, but it did help set in motion such predictable Baby Boomer hollow gestures as donning AIDS ribbons and singing songs about the *desaparecidos* and buying Rainforest Crunch. The most important thing about the Chilean wine boycott is that it typifies post-sixties Boomer activism: the ostentatious display of officially sanctioned emotions with absolutely no regard for their efficacy.

Number Four. December 3, 1967. *Ginger Baker sports the first internationally famous male ponytail.* Like the synthesizer, clog dancing, cocaine and Rod Stewart, the ponytail did not initially seem as sinister as it would later reveal itself to be. As far as can be determined, Baker, the lead-footed drummer for the original supergroup, Cream, did not sport a ponytail because he thought it would made him look better but because he wanted to keep his hair out of his eyes while he was thundering away on his double drum-kit, even though, as Buddy Rich once pointed out, a single set would have been more than adequate. Indeed, one often got the impression that Baker, who was essentially a jazz musician, though not a very good one, only grew his hair out because rock stars of the late sixties were expected to have extremely long hair.

Nevertheless, Baker is responsible for imposing the original cultural imprimatur on the male ponytail, legitimizing a hairstyle that in one form or another would plague American civilization for the next three decades and well into a fourth. This is not to say that Baker is to bear direct personal responsibility for the 2.5 million ponytailed, know-it-all, hipper-than-thou, intrusive waiters who made the dining experience sheer torture throughout the 1990s, nor can he be held directly responsible for the greasy Cali Cartel ponytail, the Steven Seagal martial arts ponytail, the salt-and-pepper Best Sound Mixing in a Documentary Short Academy Award Co-nominee ponytail, the classic Patrick Rafter the Golden Horde Rides Again ponytail, or the now all-but-forgotten Bill Walton I Just Came Down the Human Highway from the Magic Mountain ponytail, perhaps the finest example of a mercifully short-lived phenomenon: the White Jock ponytail. Finally, it would not be fair to blame Baker for the extremely popular Now-I'm-an-Investment-Banker; Now-I-Gotta-Get-My-Boogie-Down ponytail that can still be seen all over New York and Los Angeles.

Number Five. July 4, 1977. *Message T-shirts become a staple of urban fashion.* Here we come face-to-face with a case of the pernicious Law of Unintended Effects. Once upon a time, if a T-shirt spoke, it expressed a clever or amusing thought. Then one day, somebody showed up with a T-shirt that read IF YOU CAN'T IMPRESS THEM WITH YOUR INTELLECT, BURY THEM WITH YOUR BULLSHIT. This event was seminal for a number of reasons. One, it made it socially acceptable to indulge in public textual vulgarity. Two, it inaugurated an era in which feuding camps literally engaged in a chemise-based duel for platitudinal supremacy in this society. Three, it defined the moment when the individualism of the sixties gave way to the dire conformity of the seventies. From this point onward, it was no longer vital to do your own thing. Now we would all express our feelings through prefabricated banalities, clichés that someone else had already manufactured. We would go for the burn. We would accept that without pain, there could be no commensurate gain. We would just do it.

But there is more to it than that. If you rifled through many people's drawers back in the eighties you would not have found three dozen different T-shirts with three dozen different messages. No, you would have found thirty-six T-shirts in different colors carrying exactly the same message. It would be like the scene in *Batman* where Michael Keaton shows Kim Basinger his huge collection of interchangeable Batman suits. I'm a mono-platitudinous person, the shirts seemed to say, a one-banality guy in a multi-banality town. These shirts not only speak to me; they speak for me.

Number Six. June 15, 1979. Rocky II *is released.* In the early seventies, young people thought they were living through a golden age of music. In reality, they were living through a golden age of film: *The Godfather, Chinatown, Carnal Knowledge, Five Easy Pieces, M*A*S*H, The Last Detail, The Conversation.* This golden age abruptly came to an end with the release of *Rocky II.* Many people point to the release of *Star Wars* as the moment the film industry changed, because it kicked off an era of films dominated by special effects. But *Star Wars,* whatever its aesthetic fallout on the industry, was still an intelligent film. *Rocky II,* by contrast, was a film made by and for morons. In addi-

tion to officially beatifying the worst actor of his generation (Sharon Stone is the only serious competition, and she
at least is easy on the eyes), *Rocky II* is important because it
introduced the concept of virtual bravado; if white people
couldn't actually beat black people in the ring, they could
go and see white people beat black people in the ring on
the screen. (In the original *Rocky*, Stallone had not yet
worked up the nerve to let his short, talentless South
Philly mook vanquish the Muhammad Ali surrogate,
Apollo Creed.) It is still hard to believe that a film as viru-
lently, albeit subliminally, racist as *Rocky II* appeared so
shortly after the civil rights movement petered out. It
brought dishonor to an entire generation. More important,
it demonstrated that America was more than ready to go
back to the same old crap the Baby Boomers had supposedly fought to uproot: wrapping oneself in the American
flag, the myth of the lovable goombah, the subtle charm of
the seriously unlettered, the romance of the Mafia. It was a
very dark moment in American history, the darkest until
Rocky III was released.

Number Seven. November 3, 1984. *Lee Iacocca, dorkus
erectus, suddenly becomes cool.* Late in 1984 I was watching a football game in a bar in Tarrytown, New York, when
I heard a couple of thirtysomething types debating the
merits of Lee Iacocca's autobiography. The argument was
a serious one. Had Iacocca in fact saved Chrysler? Or was
he the beneficiary of a government bailout? Was he an
accessible role model? What kind of president would he
make? Couldn't the country use a guy in the White House

who knew how to crack the whip? Seriously, fellas, could it not?

Right then and there, I knew that the sixties were definitely over. For two hundred years, American businessmen had been viewed with suspicion, derision or hatred. Even the good ones. Now, in the middle of the eighties, it suddenly became fashionable for Baby Boomers to devour books by flimflam men like Iacocca, Donald Trump and T. Boone Pickens. Unlike bland *Fortune* 500 suits, the Trumps and Iacoccas were depicted as iconoclasts, cowboys, desperadoes, *mavericks*. They shot from the hip. They took lip from nobody. Not to put too fine a point on it, they were *ex-cel-lent*. This resonated with Baby Boomers, who were desperate to find a socially acceptable context for their astounding greed. The Rise of the Cutting-Edge Empty Suit prepared the way for the arrival of the Rock 'n' Roll Suit, now a staple on Wall Street, and one of the most bitter fruits of the overripe Baby Boomer harvest.

Number Eight. February 12, 1998. *Democrats vociferously defend Bill Clinton during the Monica Lewinsky scandal even though they know what a creep he is.* In the 1850s, the pro-slavery Democratic party ceded the moral high ground to the brand-new Republican party. The Republican party ceded back much of the moral high ground during the Reconstruction period, ceded quite a bit more during the Roaring Twenties, and handed over whatever few inches of terrain still remained during the McCarthy Era. Throughout the sixties, seventies and eighties the Democratic party was the home away from home for dimwit spendthrifts and thoughtful dinks like Michael Dukakis, but because of the Republican party's appalling record on civil rights and its endemic racism, the Democrats could still lay claim to a clear-cut moral superiority. Then Clinton got that blow job from Monica Lewinsky and Democrats everywhere, while admitting their revulsion at Clinton *qua* man, bit the bullet, took a dive and supported their president. From this point onward, it was impossible for former sixties activists to sit tall in the saddle of their moral high horse. If Richard Nixon or Ronald Reagan or Gerald Ford or George Bush had done one-tenth of what Bill Clinton was accused of, the Baby Boomers would have run them out of town. From this point on, voting Democratic no longer had any moral or philosophical underpinnings. It was merely fashion.

Number Nine. October 12, 1971. **Jesus Christ Superstar** *debuts*. Sure, there was *Hair* and *Godspell* and nonsense like *Oh, Calcutta!*, and, yes, Broadway was already headed downhill when Andrew Lloyd Webber arrived on the scene. But the staggering popularity of *Jesus Christ Superstar* set in motion a national nightmare from which we are not likely to emerge anytime soon. Just as the invasion of the Visigoths presaged the outrages of the Vandals and led directly to the barbarities of the Huns, *Jesus Christ Superstar* led directly to *Phantom* and *Miss Saigon* and *Les Miz* and *Sunset Boulevard* and *Jekyll and Hyde* and, of course, *Cats*. Rodgers and Hammerstein, Lerner and Loewe, Rodgers and Hart, Jerome Kern, *requiescat in pace*. Baby Boomers did not destroy the American songbook when they came of age; Bruce Springsteen and Tom Petty are at least as good as Steve and Eydie, and Frank Sinatra versus Elvis is a dead heat. But what the Boomers did to Broadway is nothing short of rape.

Number Ten. October 20, 1973. *The Arab Oil Embargo/The Energy Crisis.* Baby Boomers are usually lying when they say that they can remember where they were when Abraham and Martin and John and Bobby and Jimi and Janis and Jim died; some of them were still in diapers, and many others were dead drunk or stoned out of their gourds. But virtually all Baby Boomers can remember where they were when the energy crisis started. All of a sudden there was recession and unemployment and it was hard to get a job when you got out of college and there was a Ph.D. glut and everything was just a complete downer. The Age of Aquarius had been made possible by preposterously cheap rents and cheap food and cheap dope, but once OPEC screwed up the world economy, it was time to cut the hair, trim the Fu Manchu, dump the doobies and get serious. Revolution was out; matrixing was in. What Nixon and George Wallace and Bob Hope and Lawrence Welk had failed to accomplish in a quarter-century of round-the-clock political and cultural repression a handful of greedy Arabs had accomplished in roughly twenty minutes. Was this Jihad Canyon, or what?

OBVIOUSLY THERE ARE people who will take issue with the rankings I have presented here. Some will demand to know why John Lennon's death is not included. Or, for that matter, David Crosby's birth. Others may quibble:

Why didn't you include obvious stuff like the breakup of the Beatles? The answer: Too obvious. Lacks subtlety. Fails to penetrate beneath the surface.

Rest assured, however, that many other worthy candidates were considered. Some people may date the official death of the Baby Boomer generation from the moment people who could quote from Eldridge Cleaver's *Soul on Ice* or from Angela Davis's *If They Come in the Morning* suddenly started buying books like *Emotional Intelligence*. Others may protest that Geraldo's landing a prime-time show on NBC, the Ramones making a record with strings arranged by Phil Spector, the debut of *thirtysomething*, the cancellation of *thirtysomething*, the syndication of *thirtysomething*, the very existence of *thirtysomething* are all days that will ring in infamy, dramatically altering the landscape of the Baby Boomer generation. Still others may contend that the Baby Boomer plummet into the abyss began the day someone sent the first all-purpose letter to twenty different friends. All of these suggestions have merit. Yet in all of these instances, I determined that it was a case of better luck next time. After all, I only had ten slots.

Looking back, the most difficult decision I had to make was to omit the 1972 launching of Asylum Records. Unofficial arbiters of taste incessantly debate whether musicians reflect the values of the societies they live in, or whether they antedate them and in some sense engender them. Personally, I believe the latter. Just as it is impossible to believe that there could have been a Third Reich without Adolf Hitler, it is impossible to believe that the last thirty years would have been quite so unpleasant had Asylum

Records not provided a safe harbor for musicians like the Eagles, Joni Mitchell and Jackson Browne. I will go to my deathbed believing that the pallid, unnecessary emotions these individuals tapped into with their fiendishly non-committal music did not in fact exist before the music evoked them. I can think of no more damning indictment.

It is true that the early seventies was an era dominated by turgid art rock bands such as Yes, Asia, Ambrosia, Emerson, Lake and Palmer, and King Crimson, and that these bands have much to answer for. But the easy-listening crisis that slowly but surely tore the heart out of rock 'n' roll between 1970 and 1976 can be laid directly at the door of Asylum Records. From Jackson Browne, it was but one small step to the Eagles, and after the Eagles, nothing on the face of the earth could stand between cowering humanity and Dan Fogelberg. A famous French philosopher once said: "History is a nightmare from which mankind cannot awake." What he meant to say was: "Kenny Loggins's solo career is a nightmare from which mankind cannot awake."

5

The Man Ain't Got
No Culture

When I was a very young man, there was a popular witticism that made the rounds of this society, bringing immense amusement to the masses. Garbagemen, it seemed, were no longer comfortable with the terminology traditionally used to describe them. Henceforth, garbage-men wished to be called "sanitation engineers." "Ho-ho-ho," chuckled the entire Republic, in bad need of a good laugh. It was the first time in my life that I had been exposed to the ominous powers of euphemism.

It would not be the last.

In the three decades since the term "sanitation engineer" slipped into the parlance of the hoi polloi, Baby Boomers have made a systematic attempt to geld the English language through a poisonous mixture of cant, jargon, blather, piffle, balderdash and mush. Their primary siege engine has been a virulent brand of euphemism. Sometimes this is used for reasons of political correctness ("hardscrabble" instead of "crummy"; "challenged" instead of "stupid," "downsize" instead of "fire"); sometimes because Baby Boomers like the sound of a word even though they can only guess at its meaning ("hubris," "gravitas," "sutra," "epiphany," "au naturel"); sometimes because it enables the speaker to briefly masquerade as someone who actually knows what he's talking about ("vertical integration," "validate," "facilitate"). Because Baby Boomers are the only team players with hands-on experience in this type of prioritized interfacing, the rest of society finds it difficult to verbalize, contextualize or stay on message, since the mind-set they grew up with has in a very real sense ceased to be proactively user-friendly.

For example, when Baby Boomers use the term "centered" to describe a child, it can mean anything from "has scads of grade-A munis in his trust fund" to "takes less drugs than his peers." When the term "high maintenance" is used to describe a woman, it can mean anything from "sensitive" to "high-strung" to "coke-snorting bitch." And the term "vulnerable" can mean anything from "probably gay" to "read way too much Sylvia Plath in college."

Equally exasperating is the reliance on such unwieldy terms as "cocooning," "matrixing," "mentoring," "nesting," "plateauing" and "parenting," the proliferation of which marks the first time in human history that an entire society has been overpowered by gerunds. Bill Clinton is a master of gerundification, issuing proclamations such as "We are growing the economy," while secretly reminding himself: "My incessant partying with interns is impacting Hillary's mood—or maybe she's just PMSing."

Early on, Boomers mastered the ancient art of incantatory banality, pummeling the nation into submission through the quasi-monastic repetition of such inane expressions as "poster child," "style over substance," "on the same page," "edgy" and a wide assortment of nouns modified by the all-purpose idiocy "the mother of all." And I don't want to even talk about the incessant "utilization" of dreary sports metaphors such as "swing for the fences," "hit a home run" and "it's a slam dunk."

Late in the last millennium, I listened with amusement as an announcer on a New York classical music station rattled off a list of all the massively overplayed compositions he would like to see put into the deep freeze: Vivaldi's *The Four Seasons*, Strauss's *Also Sprach Zarathustra*, Mozart's *Eine Kleine Nachtmusik*, Orff's *Carmina Burana*, etc. Though these pieces possessed varying degrees of value in purely musical terms—Mozart, Vivaldi and Strauss clearly outgunned the hapless Orff—they had all been stripped of charm, denuded of any ability to surprise the sophisticated listener, thanks to their preposterous overuse in television commercials, movie trailers and the programs of most American classical music stations. The announcer suggested that they be temporarily retired.

I feel much the same way about the semiofficial Baby Boomer lexicon. When a member of my generation wants to impress another person with the gravity of a situation, he will invariably use the word "extraordinary." As in: "My husband is an extraordinary cook; he makes the most extraordinary *farfalle*." Because we all know that no one's husband is actually an extraordinary cook, and because there is nothing inherent in *farfalle* that would lend itself to extraordinaritude, the word "extraordinary" has now effectively been decommissioned, purged of all meaning. This is also true of the words "unique," "remarkable," "amazing," "astonishing," "wise" and "awesome," all of which have been mercilessly overused by Baby Boomers in an effort to create an arcadian verbal reality that is entirely unsupported by the facts.

For example, when a fortysomething editor at *Fortune* magazine resigned not long ago, he circulated an in-house memo declaring that he had worked with some "awesomely talented" people at *Fortune* over the years, and was really going to miss them. In fact, the last awesomely talented person to work at *Fortune* magazine was Walker Evans, and he was a photographer. What the editor meant to say was "The staff at *Fortune* isn't any worse than the staff at *Money*."

This conflicted relationship with the English language is exemplified by the repeated use of juvenile terminology in situations where it is completely inappropriate. For example, a grown man should not use the term "happy camper"; it makes him sound like a chowderhead. A grown man should definitely avoid using the expression "I am not a happy camper" when discussing a matter of some import: life, death, the loss of one's job, alimony payments. A nation in which grown men say things like "I

am not a happy camper" at momentous junctures is mani-
festly not the Shining City on the Hill that our forefathers
dreamed about.

For similar reasons, Baby Boomers would be well-
advised to stop using expiration-dated banalities such as
"street cred," "rock my world," "take a chill pill" or "my
bad," most of which will be out of fashion by the time this
paragraph has been typed. Once again, what we are witnessing is the pathological Boomer need to annex cultural
gewgaws that belong to other generations, while embarrassing an entire society in the process.

And other societies as well. Yes, once they had finished
pillaging the English language, Boomers turned their gaze
toward more fertile fields. Always a precocious bunch,
they were not content to wreck their own language. Like
Genghis Khan, already master of China, Mongolia and
Transoxania, yet now turning his eyes westward toward
Baghdad and Damascus, seeking taller minarets to topple,
more glorious mosques to raze, the Baby Boomers now
turned to the romance languages, axe in hand.

Boomers, correctly perceiving that foreign languages
had limited revenue-generating potential, never bothered
to learn them. They were the first generation in history to
produce an educated class that could not speak a single
foreign tongue, if only to correctly pronounce *"demi-glacé"*
and *"gnocchi."* But, just as with classical music and jazz,
Boomers were desirous of acquiring a sliver-thin veneer of
sophistication. This is why they developed a dangerously
eclectic, hybrid language that fuses misspelled French,
incorrect Italian, gender-insensitive Spanish and pidgin
everything-else-that-happens-to-be-lying-around into one

euphonious multicultural mess. This language is almost exclusively used in informal dining establishments and coffee bars, and is best described as *francotoscana*. It is an ingenious transmutation of ordinary and even banal foreign nouns into something vaguely *molto chic*, a patois fraught with poignancy and beauty—at least to anyone who does not have a third-grade familiarity with the languages from which it is decanted.

FOR AN AGE group that has so much to say, mostly about itself, the Baby Boomer contribution to our national oral mythology is paltry indeed. Previous generations gave us "Damn the torpedoes—full speed ahead!" "Don't fire until you see the whites of their eyes!" and "Remember the Alamo!" The best Baby Boomers could come up with is "Make love, not war," "Whatever makes you happy makes me happy" and the antiquated pseudo-proletarianism "Power to the people." Where previous generations bequeathed us "Speak softly and carry a big stick," "The only thing we have to fear is fear itself" and "We shall overcome," Baby Boomers have scraped together "Whatever goes around, comes around," "Different strokes for different folks" and "Today is the first day of the rest of your life." Previous generations immortalized "The buck stops here" and "Ask not what your country can do for you; ask what you can do for your country." Our contribution? "Keep it simple, stupid" and "Don't stop thinking about tomorrow."

Go figure.

And have a nice day.

It is hardly surprising that a generation that has produced so few good sentences should also have produced so few good writers. Contemptuous of the macho Hemingway, daunted by the inaccessible Faulkner, disoriented by the bombastic Mailer, Baby Boomer writers seem to have taken the credo "Small Is Beautiful" to heart and dedicated themselves to producing work best known for its sweeping lack of sweep. Where great American writers of the past wrestled with the major life-and-death issues (the meaning of life, the meaning of democracy, the meaning of this country), consciously endeavoring to write the great American novel, the Baby Boomer literati absolutely refused to go for the brass ring. Instead, they retreated into their gender, their ethnic group, their sexual demographic group or their individual selves. Baby Boomers have produced a number of wonderful writers (Alice McDermott, Jane Smiley, Michael Cunningham, T. C. Boyle), but these writers are essentially miniaturists. If you're looking for the Boomer Balzac—or even the Boomer Sinclair Lewis— look elsewhere.

Baby Boomers haven't fared much better in other art forms. Jenny Holzer, Barbara Krueger, David Salle, Joseph Schnabel and Jeff Koontz are not on a par with Willem de Kooning, Jackson Pollock, Jasper Johns, Roy Lichtenstein and Mark Rothko. And if Philip Glass, John Adams and John Corigliano are the best composers the Baby Boomer era has to offer, we might as well stick with Santana.

How very odd that events should have played out this way. Baby Boomers grew up despising money-grubbing philistines who lived in interchangeable split-levels in generic suburbs and had universally shared opinions and consensus values and read middlebrow books and listened to hoked-up versions of the classics and thought they were a pretty classy bunch. They sneered at their parents because they read books by Taylor Caldwell and Herman Wouk and listened to music by Percy Faith and bought records with names like *Movie Themes Go Mambo*. They ridiculed their parents' affection for musicals such as *Pal Joey* and *Pajama Game*. They deemed Mom and Pop nincompoops for making stars out of nobodies like Glenn Ford, Dorothy Lamour and Zsa Zsa Gabor, gorging themselves on Doris Day and Rock Hudson movies, and sitting on the edge of their seats whenever *Ozzie and Harriet* and *Make Room for Daddy* lit up the small screen. The Boomers were having none of this. They were going to be different.

They were different, all right. They feasted on Tom Clancy and Robert James Waller and neo-Eisenhower-era travelogues by francophiles manqués like Peter Mayle, and then persuaded themselves that Stephen King was writing the true literature of our era. They devoured lethal *bambini* music by decrepit, slumming crossover acts like Luciano Pavarotti or the insipid Andrea Bocelli, and acted as if they'd just stumbled upon Gabriel Fauré's long-lost *Missa Solemnis* or the fourteen missing passages from the *Goldberg Variations*. They filled their tiny minds with pricey twaddle like *Riverdance* and still had the nerve to upbraid their parents for enjoying Robert Goulet.

It is no accident that classical music has been in steady decline for a generation, and that the average age at symphonic concerts is now eighty-four. Classical music stirs deep emotions, and Baby Boomers do not have deep emotions. When they interest themselves in classical music, it is almost always in an ornamental fashion: harmless froufrou like Vivaldi and the Pachelbel *Canon*—Renaissance Muzak—or value-added con men like the pizzicato punk, Kennedy. Or, that old standby: prepubescent Asian violinists in whom they abruptly lose interest as soon as they grow breasts.

In a frantic bid for legitimacy, Baby Boomers are forever asking people who actually love classical music to provide them with desert island record compilations. They dream of safecracking their way into the Secret Vault of Savoir Faire, where they expect to find a list of the ten best pieces of music ever written, probably scrawled in Aramaic, which they can then force Talbot and Lourdes to listen to before they are even born, in the hope it will get them into Swarthmore. In their frantic quest to acquire *Mussorgsky for Suits*, they resemble the illiterate Charlemagne begging Alcuin of York to furnish him with a few talking points to impress his fellow Franks in the Great Mead Hall: *"I've got the money; you've got the class. Can we work out a deal here?"*

Unlike their parents, most of whom did not go to college and therefore never felt comfortable in museums, Baby Boomers *did* go to college and still feel uncomfortable in museums. We are thus witnessing the ascendancy of a previously unimaginable ruling class: *educated barbarians*. Consider the supreme example of Baby Boomer vulgarity: the art phone. Art phones constitute a naïve attempt to transmute a visceral experience into an intellectual one, to transform art into journalism, to make every picture tell a story. Even if it's a picture by Barnett Newman. The intellectual underpinning of the art phone is the Boomer belief that everything in the world can be understood if one can only get one's hands on the right information, and plenty of it. Because they are uncomfortable with anything that does not call for a programmed response, Baby Boomers have a difficult time responding to art. It is impossible for them to simply look at beautiful pictures; they have to quantify them. As the man said: They know the price of everything and the value of nothing. How's the Corot market holding up after the Nasdaq high-tech meltdown? Which is a better long-term investment: early Cezannes or late Picassos? Would a Gauguin still life be worth as much as a van Gogh if he had cut off his ear too? How much is a small Courbet going to run me? And do you have one without genitalia? It's for Megan's room.

Baby Boomers are always complaining about the dumbing down of American civilization, but for the most part it is Baby Boomers who did the dumbing down. They made the fatal mistake of confusing pop culture with real culture, leaving this civilization in tatters. Somewhere along the line, the decision was made to erase the distinction between high and low art. This was particularly noticeable in the world of film. Baby Boomers grew up worshiping Fellini, Renoir, Bergman and Truffaut, but as adults they jettisoned these titans in favor of Foreign Films Lite served up by the likes of Merchant Ivory. Even when they were trying to take a step up they were taking a step down. They mistook Woody Allen and Diane Keaton for Charlie Chaplin and Buster Keaton. They overvalued

Steven Spielberg and David Lynch and Jim Jarmusch and undervalued Martin Scorsese. And it was their generation who spawned the *Saturday Night Live* comedy industry, which has done more to ravage American civilization than anything this side of crack. The result of this hierarchical reconfiguration has been nonsense like the 1988 Clint Eastwood Film Festival at New York's Museum of Modern Art, which led directly to the even more nonsensical 2000 Oliver Stone Film Festival at the same institution. In its monthly magazine announcing the festival, MoMA described Stone as "perhaps the most audacious and least complacent filmmaker working today," declaring that movies like *JFK* "pose so many questions that they render the truth mutable."

No they don't. The truth is not mutable; that's the whole point of its being true. As the historian Steven Ambrose recently noted, what happened happened, and what didn't happen didn't happen. This is a tautology that Baby Boomers in general and Oliver Stone in particular are loath to accept. There can be no denying that Oliver Stone is a director with enormous technical gifts. Nonetheless, he is intellectually dishonest, misogynistic, a first-class crybaby, and a complete idiot. Except for the sexism charge, he's a typical Baby Boomer.

FOR ANOTHER PERSPECTIVE on the way my generation has retooled this civilization, let us examine the way Baby Boomers handle tragedy. In 1987, after a good friend died a particularly hideous death, I wrote an op-ed piece in the *New York Times* complaining about his funeral service. This is the way Baby Boomers process grief; they write op-ed pieces or, worse, read them. In the article, I chided the local priest for knowing so little about my friend's background, values, hopes, dreams. I sneered at the service's generic quality, lamenting its dependence on hollow, formulaic rituals. I wished the service had been more honest, emotional and personal.

Like many others before me, I have now learned the truth of the old saying "Be careful what you wish for." Since my friend died, I have attended any number of honest, emotional, personal funerals, most of them so foolish they made my blood run cold. Between the nitwit eulogist, the farewell home video, the flatulent sign-off music and the inappropriate clothing, funerals have devolved from sacred bonding rituals into commedia dell'arte farces. And it's only going to get worse as more Boomers pass from the scene.

The Baby Boomer desecration of funerals is a subject that has not been accorded the attention it deserves. That's probably because so much time and energy have gone into ridiculing Baby Boomer weddings. Most of us have been at the service where Brad and Tabitha harangue the wedding party with their own analgesic vows, the words of the prophets no longer deemed quite equal to the task. In fact, brain-dead vows are only part of the problem. At a Scottish-American wedding I attended, the couple made the woeful decision to invite a bagpipe player to the ceremony, where his baleful rendition of "Amazing Grace" created an ambience not unlike the scene in *Braveheart* where Mel Gibson gets drawn and quartered. I was also at a wedding reception where the groom's working-class family kept threatening to mug the culturally marooned string quartet unwisely hired for the occasion. And once, I sat and watched a videotape of a wedding in which the bride and groom showed the audience a video depicting their lives before they met each other. In other words, I had to sit in a chair for forty-five minutes and watch a videotape in which a bunch of people I did not know sat down and watched a second videotape. How Pirandellian. It made me long for the good old pre-postmodern days of the marriage feast at Cana, where the biggest worry was whether the hooch was going to run out.

But in the end, there is only so much damage that can be done at weddings, because half of them end in divorces anyway. Funerals are another matter altogether. If your first wedding turns out to be a disaster, you can always make up for it the second time around. But if your funeral is a bust, you've had it. There's no such thing as a do-over.

When I was a child, I dreaded funerals because they were terribly sad. Now I dread them because they're terrible. Having catastrophically mistaken Bill Murray's *Saturday Night Live* skit about a lounge lizard funeral emcee as a viable cultural template, Baby Boomers have transformed the traditional funeral service into a ludicrous stage show: a slapdash mixture of performance art, stand-up comedy and karaoke. Funerals are no longer somber rituals where we pay our respects to the dead. They are cabaret. They are parties, fun-fests, or what used to be known as *happenings*. They entail light shows, production numbers, props. They include professionally printed programs complete with sound and lighting credits. They involve the screening of buoyant farewell films comprising inept footage of birthday parties and college graduations that was never meant to be shown in a solemn ceremony. They feature subprofessional singers who seemingly scour the obituaries looking for a chance to cackle "Forever Young" or "Wind Beneath My Wings" over the open casket of a person who obviously had no idea what he was getting into when he died. Most important, they invariably show-case a cavalcade of material-strapped wiseguy eulogists who transform what should be a serious ritual into National Mortuary Open-Mike Night.

It is no secret that Baby Boomers have a hard time deal-ing with death. A generation whose primary cultural arti-fact is the Filofax has enormous difficulty shoehorning death into its schedule: it's inconvenient, time-consuming and stressful. *"We don't have time to die this afternoon; Caitlin has ballet."* They never could have handled the onerous demands of the Black Death: *"So much bubonic plague, so little time."* But one also senses a fundamental resentment of the arbitrariness of the universe; if *we* can get our lives running on schedule, why can't our Higher Power?

It's equally clear that Boomers are terrified by the thought of a premature, violent or otherwise untidy demise. A glance at some recent films confirms this. Between 1998 and the summer of 2000, no fewer than six major ghost movies were released by Hollywood. In each of them, a human being had met with an unexpected and, in some cases, gruesome death, and was now seeking vin-dication, justice or revenge. In *The Sixth Sense*, Bruce Willis plays a dead psychiatrist who cannot report to The Afterlife for reassignment until he has atoned for a disastrous patient diagnosis that in fact led to his own demise. In *Stir of Echoes,* a raped and strangled teen refuses to evacuate the house where she was murdered until her killers have been brought to justice. In *What Lies Beneath,* it's a murdered coed seeking revenge; in *The Haunting,* it's a bunch of murdered children desperate for vindication; in *Sleepy Hollow,* it's a headless ghost seeking his head. In each case, the dead person refuses to go to his eternal reward until things have reached a satisfactory conclusion back here on planet Earth, because any other denouement would suggest that life is meaningless and that death is capricious, haphazard and stupid. The subliminal message of these motion pictures is always the same: *Just because you're dead doesn't mean you can't get your life organized.*

One would have thought that the Final Solution, the rape of Nanking, the Mongol invasions, the fall of the Roman Empire and just about all of human history would have given Baby Boomers a hint that death can be not only a bit messy, but entirely without rhyme or reason. But no, Baby Boomers have decided otherwise: The universe may seem a smidgen incoherent on first glance, but if you roll up your sleeves and attack the problem energetically you can vastly simplify your life. Or death. And one way to accomplish this is through memorable, upbeat funerals.

It must be recalled that ever since the bloodbath known as the sixties, Baby Boomers have lived in constant fear of anything that threatens to be a downer, a bad scene or what is technically known as "a drag." They don't like somber funeral services with dim lights and organ music because such grim rituals create the sense that . . . well . . . *did somebody just die in here or what?* The assumption being that the dead party wouldn't want to do anything to depress his friends. So hey, everybody, let's keep it light. Just have fun with it. Put some more scented oil on the stiff. He ain't dead; he's just mellow.

Unsurprisingly, the search for a death that everyone else can live with has already turned into an industry in some parts of America. "Home deathing" is no longer a novelty; innumerable classes on improving the overall quality of the death experience have sprung up. In San Francisco, people pay $150 for a two-day workshop at the Zen Hospice to learn how to be a compassionate "death companion." The Hospice even has plans to launch a program that will "certify" professional death companions, known as "midwives for death" or "mentors through dying," a role previously handled by the Mafia. As one alternative funeral industry bigwig told the *Wall Street Journal*, their clients "want to personalize and take control of the death experience."

To personalize and take control of the death experience—much as they had earlier personalized and taken control of the urban caffeine experience—Baby Boomers have had to perform some massive retooling of human history. Specifically, they had to throw the Past overboard. Although Boomers are aware that something loosely identified as the Past exists, they have devoted most of their adult lives to pretending that it does not. Contrary to Billy Joel's predictably inaccurate assertion that "we didn't start the fire," Baby Boomers fervently believe that they did, in fact, start the fire, that the world was an incoherent mess before they got here. The Past is nothing more than a series of incomprehensible mistakes, inhabited by people of dubious taste and questionable judgment who do not measure up as human beings when compared to such remarkable people as, say, us.

The way Baby Boomers see it, George Washington and Thomas Jefferson were incorrigible racists whose incidental contributions to the birth of this great nation are completely overshadowed by the mighty deeds of a Martin Luther King or even a Richard Gere. Shakespeare was an anti-Semite, Hemingway a homophobe, Emily Dickinson a wacko, and Mark Twain used the "N-word." None of them are in the same class as Susan Sarandon. Via determinations such as this, Baby Boomers are incessantly heaping derision on the Past in order to justify their fatuous innovations in the Present. And the Past cannot fight back.

Previous generations—say, every single generation dating back to 10,000 B.C.—recognized that history was a fungible resource. They believed that you could learn important things from your forebears: Refrain from sticking your hands in a roaring fire, never let small children play on Mount Vesuvius, think twice before declaring war on the Roman Empire. Then Baby Boomers came along. Adopting a sort of pop Maoism they decided that society must be in a state of permanent upheaval, that its most venerable codes must be repeatedly tested, its traditions reevaluated, its rituals discarded, transmogrified or reinvented. Nowhere is the fallout from this mind-set more apparent than in the treatment of tragedy.

Start with the lingo. On Saturday, July 8, 2000, newspapers all over America carried reports of the death of Cory Erving, the eighteen-year-old son of basketball immortal Julius Erving. Cory, who had been missing for several weeks, had finally been found dead in a pond not far from the Erving house. Upon receiving this horrible news, Julius Erving issued the following statement: "We are thankful to the Seminole County Sheriff's Office for bringing Cory back to us. We now have resolution. Getting closure was very important to the family in coping with the loss." He added: "We have learned a lot from this tragedy, and we will be a stronger family as a result. The Erving family will go forward from here. We have no other choice."

With all due respect to Erving, this vacuous statement is quintessential Boomer blather. Our parents and their parents and everyone's parents were brought up to believe that when a child dies, the whole universe screams. But Baby Boomers are so uncomfortable with the language of grief that they have invented an official funereal twaddle for dealing with precisely such occasions. Tragedy thus becomes another opportunity for character development. A police visit or lake dredging or autopsy brings us resolution. Instead of raging against the dying of the light, we are happy for closure. King Lear, we are not.

OVER THE COURSE of human history, most societies wisely developed a priestly class whose job it was to preside over important rituals—many of them unpleasant—and say what needed to be said in words that would offend the smallest number of people. Not surprisingly, their most important work was done at funerals. Though priests and rabbis and ministers and shamans and even charismatic witch doctors could sometimes rise to the occasion and wax poetic, their basic mission was to hew close to society's most treasured platitudes, providing reassurance to the grieving parties that death was part of life, that life itself had structure and purpose, that death was not a capricious, arbitrary, meaningless or especially unpleasant event.

Obviously, much of what the clerical class had to say was nonsense, but for the first five thousand years of recorded history this didn't seem to bother anyone. Society at some subconscious level seemed to recognize that even though the high priest could be dull and repetitive and verbose and even vindictive, this was still preferable to letting laymen get into the act. In the course of evolution from shrub-gnawing apes to Sting, societies as diverse as the Mayans, the Maoris and the Jutes seemed to have agreed on one common point: Funerals are already depressing enough, so let's not make things worse by letting the guy who thinks he's Gallagher speak at the service.

Then along came the Baby Boomers. Convinced of their eloquence, unbending in their belief that they had something to say that nobody else had ever thought of before, Boomers decided that religious figures needed to be purged from the funeral ceremony, or at least marginalized. The result is one of the worst innovations in the history of remorse: the tag-team eulogy. This is the funeral ceremony where as many as two dozen friends of the deceased get up in the pulpit and share their thoughts about the person being buried. Baby Boomers seem incapable of understanding that people attending funerals generally share the same emotions, making it unnecessary for twelve different people to say how much they are going to miss the creature in the casket or urn. But no, everyone has to get up and thank the dead person for "being there."

One funeral I attended featured nine different eulogist headliners. Most of them did a fairly good job under the circumstances; they were funny, tender, warm, affectionate. But one aspiring Mark Antony had to opt for Door Number Three. He chose to recount a conversation he'd had with his now-departed friend shortly before he died. The deceased had recently recovered from a long illness and was now on the mend. He had a new job that he genuinely enjoyed. He was working on a raftload of exciting projects that had recently been moved off the back burner. He honestly believed that he had turned the corner and was very excited about what life held in store for him. Then he died. The eulogist concluded this reverie with the words: "It reminds me of that old saying: If you want to make God laugh, tell him about your plans."

This philosophical bon mot constitutes what used to be known as a "bummer" or a "bring down." The speaker has already established his personal bona fides, demonstrating beyond a shadow of a doubt that he has standing to speak about the deceased. He has beguiled the mourners with his witty repartee and a tasteful assortment of colorful anecdotes. He has opened his heart; he has shared. Now all he needs to do is to get off the stage. But no, he has to push the envelope. First, despite the fact that this is a rigorously nonsectarian service, he has to get in a little dig at the Creator. This always gets things off to a good start. Then, whether he is aware of it or not, he goes out of his way to show disrespect for the person he has come to eulogize. *What a jerk you were for thinking you were finally getting your act together! Don't you know that this is an indif-*

ferent universe, where life is meaningless and death even more so? Don't you know how things work on this planet? Jesus Christ Almighty, what is it with you?"

Maybe it's time for funeral directors to start vetting these speeches.

Another unfortunate Baby Boomer contribution to the mortuary arts is the theologically eclectic funeral service. It has long been my belief that people should be buried in the rites of the religion least likely to embarrass them. But because Baby Boomers are all over the lot philosophy-wise, I have often had to attend services where the various liturgies not only war with each other but sometimes cancel one another out. Because we Baby Boomers believe in nothing, we end up acting like we believe in everything. Funeral services thus become a religious smorgasbord. This is not good.

Personally speaking, once I've heard the sparse Quaker prayer and the lugubrious Kaddish reading and a couple of unpublished poems by some tribal elder from Manitoba, I've don't have the energy left to gut out the Seventh Sutra of the Sun. Often I come away from these services more confused and saddened than when I went in. First, I'm told that my friend is just another form of energy. Then I find that he's up there looking down on us. No, that's not right, he's gone to a far, far better place. No, his spirit is breathing in the daffodils just outside the window. No, he's stone fucking dead, so get used it. One time I was so distraught upon returning from a spectacularly multicultural funeral that I went into my closet, yanked out a baseball bat, and handed it to my fourteen-year-old son.

"Gord, I want you to make me a promise," I said. "I want you to promise me that when I die, if anyone gets up at my funeral and mentions the I Ching, the Bhagavad-Gita or the Tibetan Book of the Dead, or if anyone even so much as suggests that I am not dead but have just transmuted myself into another form of energy, or if anyone implies that I was just chomping at the bit to meet my Maker, that I felt a tremor of bliss, that in those last weeks and months I almost seemed to be letting go, then please take this baseball bat and break their motherfucking legs. And if anyone dares to mention the word 'sutra' at my funeral you have my permission to kill them."

"Cool," was my son's reply.

IN MY PERHAPS outmoded view, for a funeral to truly work two things are necessary. First off, a modicum of respect must be shown. Here I am talking about contemporary funeral attire. Last year, I attended a service where two middle-aged men were wearing New York Giants windbreakers. No matter who is being buried, this is unacceptable mourning garb. For one, it's tasteless and shows a lack of breeding. Two, the Giants finished 6–10 that season and didn't even make the playoffs. What kind of message does that send to the kids? Or to the dead person? The lesson to be learned is simple: If you don't care enough about the dearly departed to put on a suit and a tie, then stay home. This is doubly true for Cleveland Browns fans.

Second, it is necessary for at least one person to admit that he is actually going to miss the dead person. I am not suggesting that we need to go overboard, with the rending of clothing and the tearing of hair and the gnashing of teeth. But for a dead person to get the send-off he deserves, at least one person actually has to break down and cry. If it is not possible for the mother, children or significant other to do this, I suggest that survivors start hiring official mourners to provide an aura of grief at funerals. I am sure they can be found in Northern California. One of my friends has even suggested holding two funerals for every person that dies: one for the weepy types, the rest for the mourners on Prozac. Of course, there are always those who make a point of never attending funeral services, because, as they so cleverly put it, "I don't do grief." For them, e-funerals should do very well indeed.

6

What a Fool Believes

One day in the spring of 1984, Tom Brokaw was strolling along a beach in Normandy, France, when it suddenly dawned on him that his parents' generation rocked big-time. Though he kept this opinion to himself until Tim Russert broached the subject ten years later on *Meet the Press*, and though he never actually used the expression "rocked big-time," Brokaw had already run the numbers and made up his mind: The Americans born circa 1920, who had defeated the Nazis, the Japanese and the rest of those fascist head cases, and who had then gone on to build the most dynamic economy the world has ever known, constituted "the greatest generation any society has ever produced."

Mind you, Brokaw did not say "the greatest generation of the century." Nor did he say "the greatest generation in American history." Nor did he say "the greatest generation since the Renaissance." No, in Brokaw's view, the folks who brought you Glenn Miller, Benny Goodman, the Boys of Summer, the Thunderbird, split-level houses and the Battle of the Bulge, as well as Shecky Green, Joe McCarthy, Jimmy Durante and Sans-a-Belts were *the greatest generation ever to inhabit this extraordinary planet.*

Nevertheless, Brokaw had a sense that there was something paradoxical about the stunning record of the Greatest Generation. Given how stupendously heroic they were, what with single-handedly preventing the Spawn of Satan from permanently extinguishing the floodlights of civilization and whatnot, they had certainly kept an amazingly low profile. Despite their impressive achievements, Brokaw shamefacedly had to admit that he had, up until now, somehow managed to overlook their accomplishments.

As he put it: "I realized that they [the Greatest Generation Any Society Has Ever Produced, henceforth referred to as the GGASHEP] had been all around me as I was growing up and that I had failed to appreciate what they had been through and what they had accomplished." This depressed him. It puzzled him. And finally it galvanized him. Determined that the mighty deeds of the GGASHEP not be dismissed as a mere footnote to history, Brokaw now decided to write a powerful testament, called *The Greatest Generation.*

Brokaw is to be congratulated for his heart-swelling paean to the men and women who came of age during the Great Depression. Those who knew them, those who loved them, those who fought them and most especially those who actually were them would wholeheartedly agree with his assertion that, as a demographic package, the Greatest Generation were the cat's meow and the bee's knees rolled into one.

Yet it is no disservice to the distinguished newsman and his industrious team of researchers to suggest that they got to the party late. Putting it bluntly, Brokaw's revelations about the extraordinary heroism of his parents' generation was not exactly stop-the-presses material. Several movies and books had been written between 1945 and the present on the subject of the Second World War, and most of them had mentioned the fact that the Allied Forces were pretty darned courageous. Also, it was widely acknowledged—at least among people who had finished two years of college—that the defeat of the Nazis, the greatest threat to Western Civilization since the Mongols blew through town in the thirteenth century, was a very important event.

In addition, about half the people in the United States had grown up in households headed by people who had lived through the Great Depression and who had fought in the Second World War and who couldn't go five minutes without talking about either of these seminal events. So it wasn't as if Team Brokaw had stumbled upon some amazing, consensus-altering secret (the Brontë sisters were cannibals, the ancient Phoenicians invented Tetris,

Willa Cather was into leather, Moses was a blind, bisexual dwarf).

Given this context, I began reading *The Greatest Generation* from a somewhat jaundiced perspective. Although there was something sweet and innocent about Brokaw's "discovery" that the people who won the Second World War were a remarkable group of people, I felt that in making this assertion Brokaw had inadvertently tipped off his readers to the fact that he was not much of a history buff. Look at it this way: If the Greatest Generation was, indubitably, the Greatest Generation, then why had it only just dawned on him? How was it possible for the Greatest Generation Any Society Has Ever Produced to stay out of the spotlight until the vaunted newsman was already well into his fifties? Was the competition from other generations and other societies that strong? Had there been some kind of conspiracy—perhaps involving the United Nations, black helicopters, or the Trilateral Commission—to conceal the GGASHEP's greatness? Or was the GGASHEP so incredibly self-effacing that the rest of us hadn't even noticed them until they were already shuffling off history's garish stage?

Most people with a college education can rattle off the causes of the Peloponnesian War, explain in detail why Caesar's crossing the Rubicon was so important, and also have a pretty fair handle on why the beheading of Louis XVI was such a major historical event. Somehow, I doubt that Brokaw has this information at his fingertips. Which is why one has to call into question his assertion that his parents' peers formed the Greatest Generation Any Society Has Ever Produced. Since the English had already won the Battle of Britain by the time the United States bothered to enter the war, I suspect that he's going to get some quibbling from the folks in Old Blighty regarding the title of Most Heroic People Ever. And if the standard of greatness is a generation's military performance against the forces of evil, then the Russians, who lost 10 million men to our 450,000, and won the most important battle of the war (Stalingrad), have to get the nod as the most gallant, courageous, and inexpendable warriors of all time. As a famous man once said, the Second World War was won by English courage, American money and Russian blood. I believe the author of this remark was Winston Churchill, a man in a better position to know than Tom Brokaw.

Of course, Brokaw would probably argue that it was building an industrial colossus *after* having defeated the Nazis that qualified his parents as the Greatest Generation Any Society Has Ever Produced. But here again there is ample room for debate. America had already been the richest nation in the world for about seventy-five years by the time the Greatest Generation showed up. Despite the reverses of the Depression, the infrastructure of greatness was already in place by the time the GGASHEP arrived on the scene. By contrast, previous generations (say, the Pilgrims) had to start from scratch. Why had Brokaw so cavalierly overlooked their amazing accomplishments?

And what about Europe and Asia? Surely any generation that produced Sophocles, Pericles and Euripides must be worthy of some consideration here. Surely Augustus Caesar and his Roman contemporaries, men and women who created an empire that lived on in one form or another for fifteen hundred years, are entitled to a few votes. Surely the Franks who defeated the Huns, the Italians who gave us the Renaissance, the Elizabethan English, the Enlightenment French, the Dutch Masters all merit some serious review. Not to mention the generation that produced Jesus Christ, the single most important man who ever lived, like it or not.

Little by little, I began to suspect that when Brokaw attempted to deify his parents' generation as the Greatest Generation Any Society Has Ever Produced, he may have been guessing. After all, he had to tell Tim Russert *something*.

The more I turned things over in my head, the more I was forced to admit that Brokaw had willfully insulted an awful lot of dead people who had at least as worthy a claim to the mantle of greatness as the Folks Who Brought You the Cha-Cha. It's one thing to build a greater society after someone has already handed you a starter great society. It's another thing to put those first points on the scoreboard. George Washington, Thomas Jefferson, John Adams, Alexander Hamilton, Betsy Ross, Nathan Hale, Molly Pitcher and Paul Revere all put their heads in a noose so that people like Tom Brokaw could make a fortune off books they'd pieced together on subjects they didn't seem to know much about. Five hundred thousand young men born in 1840 or thereabouts had given their lives at Gettysburg and Missionary Ridge and Antietam so that Johnny-come-latelies like Brokaw could belatedly kiss their parents' asses and make a few bucks on the side. And the doughboys gassed and blinded at Ypres and Beaulieu

Woods had also given a pretty fair account of themselves in a war that was actually more cataclysmic in a paradigm-shifting sense than the Second World War. Yet Brokaw had blithely chosen to ignore the obvious greatness of these heroic individuals.

Why?

The obvious answer: He is a product of the Baby Boomer Era. Baby Boomers (Brokaw, born in 1940, technically misses the cut, but he is awarded Honorary Boomer status here, not only because most of his peers are Boomers, but because his persona embodies everything we have come to identify with this generation) instinctively assume that everything important that ever happened in the entire history of the universe had to have happened in their lifetime. In their view, the Beatles are greater than Ellington, Mark McGwire is more dangerous than Babe Ruth, and Joe Montana is better than Johnny Unitas. Anything that happened in the more distant past doesn't quite measure up. Delacroix? Talented, but no Andy Warhol. Attila the Hun? A player, but no Saddam Hussein. Edgar Allan Poe? Facile, but lacks the majestic sweep of Stephen King. This is the most plausible explanation for Brokaw's ill-considered historical ranking system. He was on a talk show with Tim Russert, he kind of got put on the spot, he looked around for the Greatest Generation Any Society Has Ever Produced, he correctly saw that it wasn't his own, so he just naturally assumed that it had to have been his parents'. Otherwise, the universe made no sense.

There is another, more plausible explanation for Brokaw's oversight. On page viii, in acknowledging the authors to whose work he is indebted, Brokaw listed a scant five names. They were: William Manchester, Paul Fussell, Ben Bradlee, Andy Rooney and Art Buchwald. Conspicuously absent were Alan Bullock, A. J. P. Taylor, Jules Michelet, Edward Gibbon, Tacitus, Thucydides, Plutarch and Herodotus, all of whom might have pitched in and helped out. The presence of the names Andy Rooney and Art Buchwald in this bibliographical compendium is particularly telling; it shows that Brokaw is not afraid of being sneered at, nor does he dread allegations that his research is a smidgen less than thorough. Again, a typical Baby Boomer attitude. History is bunk. Which is why I never bothered to learn any.

SHORTLY AFTER I read *The Greatest Generation*, I happened upon an angry screed in *Esquire* entitled "The Worst Generation." The jeremiad had been written by Democratic political operative Paul Begala, another self-loathing Baby Boomer as well. In obvious response to Brokaw's work, Begala identified his fellow Boomers as the worst generation in American history, citing such crimes as selfishness, greed, cowardice and the invention of disco.

I enjoyed Begala's article much more than Brokaw's book, in part because I had every reason to believe that he had written it all by himself. Yet in the end, I was no more satisfied with his hysterical rant than I was with Brokaw's quite serious, albeit ill-conceived, premise. It was true that Baby Boomers were venal, hypocritical, self-absorbed, greedy, intellectually dishonest and, in many ways, cowardly. Nor could it be denied that they invented disco. But they also invented punk, which canceled out disco. And when Begala attempted to exonerate Bill Clinton of his crimes, substituting George W. Bush as the archetypal Boomer, he lost me.

Still, the article provided food for thought. It was true that our parents had survived the Great Depression, defeated the Nazis, and built the American industrial empire. It was also true that when the generations went head to head, the results were not pretty. They had John Kennedy; we had Michael Kennedy. They had Robert Kennedy; we had Patrick Kennedy. They had Joseph Kennedy; we had Kennedy. They had Lucky Luciano; we had Lucky Vanous. They had Jackson Pollock; we had Jackson Browne. They had Kirk Douglas; we had Michael Douglas. They had Sonny Rollins; we had Sonny Bono. They had Miles Davis; we had Miles Copeland. They had Bird; we had the Eagles. They had the Count and the Duke; we had the Artist Formerly Known as Prince. They had Our Lady of Fatima; we had Madonna and Lourdes. Game, set, match: They cleaned our clock.

Despite this, it has recently become a cliché to go completely overboard, as Begala did, and describe Baby Boomers as the most appalling generation in American history. In fact, my very decision to use the *Spy* house adjective "appalling" is a perfect example of the rehearsed hyperbole that is typical of my generation, since we are the generation that replaced cloying sincerity with studied archness, and since I used to write archly for *Spy*. Moreover, most of the journalists excoriating Baby Boomers are themselves Baby Boomers, so their rancor is just another way of placing themselves at the very epicenter of the Circle of Life.

It goes without saying that Baby Boomers are venal, hypocritical, self-absorbed egomaniacs blighted by an insalubrious interest in things like the provenance of their neighbors' balsamic vinegar. But this does not make them monsters; it merely makes them *annoying*. Baby Boomers did not distribute blankets infected with smallpox to American Indians, they did not wipe out the buffalo, they did not swell the Ku Klux Klan's ranks to four million strong as happened in 1924, and they did not make a habit of blowing up churches with small children inside them the way the so-called Greatest Generation did back in the fifties. Baby Boomers, whatever their faults, did not invent Richard Nixon or George Wallace or Sammy Davis, Jr., or burgundy polyester pants suits or white patent leather shoes or Howard Cosell or Florida retirement communities where seniors could run off and pretend that the emotionally responsive portion of their lives was over. For that matter, they did not invent Andy Rooney and Art Buchwald. To describe them as the worst generation ever is merely to take the calculating, market-driven Brokawian thesis that our parents were the greatest generation ever (fat chance!) and stand it on its head. In other words, to pull the classic Boomer stunt of being puckishly clever while being completely wrong.

At this juncture, it is critical to bring some perspective to the cross-generational wars and place Baby Boomers in their proper historical context. In reality, as almost everyone knows, George Washington's generation and the generation that fought the Civil War far outstrip the generation that won the Second World War, while Baby

Boomers rank somewhere in the bottom middle: not quite as noteworthy as the generation that won World War I, but certainly no worse than the generation that came of age in the 1840s and 1880s, and probably not as bad as Generation X, who showed up on the scene too late with too little. If nothing else, Baby Boomers are good at making money. And making money is what America is all about.

One reason pronouncements like Brokaw's are so blatantly foolhardy is because great developments in world history can never be chalked up to a single generation. The other fallacy inherent in his argument lies in the fact that different generations accomplish different things at different points in their lives. When the Revolutionary War broke out, Benjamin Franklin was almost seventy, George Washington was in his forties, Thomas Paine was thirty-eight, Thomas Jefferson thirty-two, and Alexander Hamilton was not yet twenty. Which generation gets credit for midwifing the United States? Franklin's for providing its most revered statesman? Washington's for producing the indispensable military leader? Paine's for furnishing the rabble-rouser? Jefferson's for supplying a man capable of doing the important paperwork? Or Hamilton's for figuring out a way to pay the infant republic's bills?

The very same case can be made with the GGASHEP. Who was the single most important American in the years 1900–1950, during which the GGASHEP were performing their miraculous deeds? Franklin Delano Roosevelt. He was born in 1882. He showed up forty-two years too early to belong to the GGASHEP.

- - - - -

WHERE THEN DO the Baby Boomers rank among the generations in history? Based on my exhaustive research, I've got them 267th all-time, right behind the Carthaginians born in 220 B.C., and just slightly ahead of the Japanese born during the Yoritomo Shogunate in A.D. 1192. Closer to home, if we accept the popular thesis presented by Neil Howe and William Strauss in their 1990 book, *Generations*, that there have been fourteen generations since the American Revolution, then I've got the Baby Boomers tied for the No. 9 slot. They do not compete with the generation born in 1760, which got the country up and running, nor with the generation of 1840, which fought the Civil War. As already discussed, they are also not in a class with the generation that fought the Second World War (or the First), nor with the generation born in 1860, which built the great industrial colossus known as the United States.

But they are vastly superior to the generations born in 1800 and 1820, which failed to deal with the slavery issue that was tearing the country apart, and they are at least the equal of the generation born in 1880, which was vulgar and greedy and complacent and dull. At this point, Baby Boomers are still far ahead of Generation X, though that could change in the future when Generation X actually accomplishes something. However, that will probably not occur before this book is published.

In assessing the achievements of the Baby Boomers vis-à-vis the Greatest Generation, there is one matter that remains to be addressed. For a generation to be considered truly great, it isn't enough to defeat the combined forces of Satan and Moloch or to build a mighty industrial empire the likes of which the world has never known. It is also necessary to transmit your values to your descendants. *Transmit*, and not merely bequeath. This was one of the great failings of Marcus Aurelius; he was a beloved emperor, a gifted writer, a cogent, important philosopher and a superb human being. Yet he bequeathed his empire to his son, Commodus, a monster.* Which means that in some sense, and indeed in a rather large sense, he failed. The same argument can be made about Edward I, the dreaded Hammer of the Scots, whose son, Edward II, was a complete ninny; about Henry V, whose son, Henry VI, was an idiot; about Augustus Caesar, whose successors, almost without exception, were perverts or madmen; and about Andrew Jackson, whose handpicked successor was the sly but ineffectual Martin Van Buren. So my final question to Tom Brokaw is simple: *If the Greatest Generation was so great, how come they raised children like the Baby Boomers?*

---

*For more information on this subject, consult Edward Gibbon's *The Decline and Fall of the Roman Empire*, Bertrand Russell's *A History of Western Philosophy* or Ridley Scott's *Gladiator*.

7

Careful, the Staff Might Hear You

In the previous chapter, I oh-so briefly contrasted the achievements of Baby Boomers with the generation that followed them. In doing so, I knew whereof I spoke. Before sitting down to write this book, I conducted lengthy interviews with a statistically meaningful number of Gen Xers to unearth their true feelings about Baby Boomers. Without exception, they wished we would all die. When I asked why, they invariably cited Baby Boomers' monstrous self-absorption and inability to perceive their own "lameness," the latter being both a function of and a verification of the former. When I asked for

more specific complaints, they cited many of the transgressions listed in the first two chapters of this book, but
also mentioned the following:

- Baby Boomers are embarrassing the entire
  nation through their misguided obsession
  with remaining *youthful* in both appearance
  and behavior in spite of the biological facts
  and social imperatives working against them.
  Traditionally, older people in most societies
  have functioned as wise, respected mentors to
  younger generations. But how could any
  young person today possibly take advice from
  a fifty-three-year-old man wearing a baseball
  cap turned backward, perched on roller
  blades, who is contemplating a stint at Burning Man?
- They grew up saying that the suburbs are sterile, but now they all live there and insist that
  the suburbs are America's best-kept secret.
- They actually use expressions like "America's
  best-kept secret."
- They annex, colonize, co-opt or steal everything—fashion, music, language, beverages—
  that belongs to other generations.
- They don't ever actually want anything. They
  just want a huge number of choices.
- They had one formative experience in their
  youth that they never stop talking about.
  Either they spent their junior year in Kabul or
  they slept with a Gurkha or they once dated a

deaf, dark-skinned security guard in Fresno, and that was their big thrill for their entire life. They always act like nobody else ever dated a deaf, dark-skinned security guard in Fresno or like everybody else secretly wished that they had spent their junior year in Kabul.

- They belong to expensive gyms whose annual membership fees would be sufficient to feed a family of Ethiopians for a week.

- They sheepishly joke about belonging to ridiculously expensive gyms whose annual fees would be sufficient to feed a family of Ethiopians for a week, as if this backhanded admission of guilt makes the Ethiopians feel any better.

- They talk about the injuries they have sustained in their overpriced gyms, as if anybody could possibly care.

- They have to go everywhere and experience everything.

- Their heroes are all fakes (Abbie Hoffman, Jerry Rubin, Jane Fonda, William Kunstler).

- They've become just like their parents. They're old, mean, greedy, self-centered and terribly disappointed in their kids.

- They got teargassed once, then went to work for Goldman Sachs. But they still think that beneath that investment banker's suit beats the heart of a rebel. They all secretly believe that they'll run off and join Shining Path when their kids are out of college.

- They have to videotape everything.
- They believe in the transformative power of yoga.
- They have bottomless faith in self-help, though it's obviously not working.
- They use words like "centered" and act surprised when people want to assassinate them for it.
- Everyone important to the Boomers got shot or strangled on his own puke.
- They act like if you missed Woodstock you might as well have never been born, even though they all missed Woodstock.
- They use sporting analogies for everything, even though they were never any good at sports.
- They use military analogies for everything, even though they were never in the army.
- They act like they're the only people who ever had a bad airline experience.
- They insist that everything have a nickname. Like "Baby Boomers."
- They believe that everything is part of a larger trend that only they can see.
- They enthusiastically embrace every trend, and then when the trend becomes ridiculous, they deny that they ever had anything to do with it.
- They are always asking things like whether the coffee in the diner is any good. It's diner coffee; what do you think, asshole?

- They will not and cannot shut up about themselves.

MUCH AS I appreciated this material, I came away from my interviews feeling that those who had cast so many stones were not themselves entirely without sin. For starters, Gen Xers tend to act as if their generation has no overlap with Boomers. This is not true. The two generations interface and interact and even collude all the time. Indeed, one subject that has rarely been examined is the unofficial, unholy alliance between Baby Boomers and Gen Xers.

Although Boomers and slackers profess to despise each other, in many ways they are more like Serbs and Croatians, implacable enemies who occasionally suspend hostilities and join forces *brazo a brazo* to make life miserable for the Bosnians. If, for the purposes of this conversation, we think of our figurative Bosnians as consisting of older people, Gen Yers, small children, foreigners or anyone who is technically a Baby Boomer or a Gen Xer but who secretly hates his generation (this would probably apply to most readers of this book), one gets a much more precise image of the victimized class of which I speak.

Clearly, there are a number of areas where Baby Boomers and Gen Xers have pooled their resources to make society unbearable for everyone else. Whiny, jingly-jangly bands like R.E.M. may appeal much more to slackers than to their own generation, but they are still basically Tail End Boomers who sound an awful lot like the Byrds. In fact, virtually all "alternative" bands sound like the Byrds, except for the ones that sound like the Ramones.

Blues Traveler is a Gen X reincarnation of the blustery, plodding Blood, Sweat and Tears, just as the Black Crowes are a Gen X retread of Humble Pie, Aerosmith, Led Zeppelin, the Stones—basically everybody. Burning Man is the Men's Movement with Slightly Less Afrocentric Music. Gen X yuppie scum are no different from Boomer yuppie scum; they have Ikea, we had Crate & Barrel. Elitist Web sites like *Salon*'s vile "Mothers Who Think" may have been launched by Gen Xers, but the attitude is pure Baby Boomer: If you don't agree with mothers like us, it's because mothers like you lack a brain. You Republican cunts.

Another classic example of intra-generational collusion: coffee bars, which fuse the Gen X passion for micro-pleasures with the Baby Boomer demand for unlimited choice in a hideously pretentious and overpriced environment where every product's name is derived from Pig Italian. Also cell phones, one of the most obnoxious inventions in all of human history, allow whining Gen Xers to bore everyone in the general vicinity with the details of their dull, low-paying jobs, while enabling smarmy Baby Boomers to bore everyone between Coral Gables and Butte with the details of their absolutely fabulous careers and Karena's first lacrosse game. The result is the same: Decent people suffer. Last but not least, the Internet is a quintessential Gen X–Baby Boomer collaboration: Let's fill our existence with even more minutiae that we can never stop talking about and act like it's going to improve our undernourished lives.

The two most vexatious generations to ever grace the

planet have also collaborated on the evisceration of the English language, each mass-producing an incessant stream of banalities that the other generation immediately adopts, refines, co-opts or purloins. "Not." "As if." "Edgy." "Out of control." "Go figure." "Do the math." "Don't go there." "I'm outta here." "Awesome." "Excellent." "Totally." Every few weeks I get an e-mail from a natural products company called GreenMarketplace.com. I ended up on their list while researching my last book, which poked fun at do-gooders. To unsubscribe from this list—"unsubscribe" being another of those ghastly neologisms coined by earnest young people who had originally vowed to make the world a more beautiful place—the company advises:

> Please go to
> <AHREF="http://www.greenmarketplace.com/greenmarket/mailinglist/subs.html">http://www.greenmarketplace.com/greenmarket/mailinglist/subs.html</A>.

Yes, the Internet's going to be a big help.

AND THEN THERE is the difficult subject of transcontinental irony. While it is true that Baby Boomers invented the idea of irony as a preemptive emotion, as a handy baffling device to prevent the white noise coming in from Rwanda, Serbia, Cabrini Green or their parents from invading their space, it is Gen Xers who have perfected the use of irony by turning it into an all-encompassing lifestyle (ironic clothing, ironic furniture, ironic childhood heirlooms as household furnishings, ironic eyeglasses, Martini culture, neo-Swingers).

It is in the irony sphere that one generation's negatively symbiotic relationship with the other is most apparent; Boomers are the virus, Gen X is the host. By providing Gen Xers with masses of pop cultural artillery, Boomers have ensured that this society will spend the next quarter-century drowning in cheap irony. First, Baby Boomers produced or popularized monstrosities like *The Brady Bunch, Gilligan's Island*, ABBA, disco, polyester and other entities that were initially, quite correctly, identified as being idiotic. Then, inevitably, Baby Boomers became mildly nostalgic for the detritus of their youth. Sensing an opening, Gen Xers moved in and embraced *The Brady Bunch, Gilligan's Island*, ABBA, disco and polyester, smirking to one another that because pathetic Baby Boomers were oblivious to the ironic subtext underpinning this mass conversion, Gen X had thereby landed a body blow on the overlords who oppress them on a daily basis. Even though Baby Boomers were unaware of this deft subversive attack, because they were too busy with their own ironic endeavors, and therefore largely impervious to irony concocted by other generations.

Meanwhile, the Greatest Generation looks at their watches and wonder how much longer the Grim Reaper's going to be, because this whole damn society has gone to hell in an irony-suffused, deeply postmodern handbasket.

Sometimes, Gen Xers borrow ironic things from Baby Boomers and then Baby Boomers borrow them back. This makes life hopelessly confusing. The end result is that the two groups have introduced so many levels of irony that it is impossible for a non-ironic or irony-neutral person or foreigner or senior citizen or small child to figure out what is what anymore.

Here is an example. One day I was out for a ride on my bicycle when I decided to stop in a suburban cafeteria that was not affiliated with any of the major franchises. As I entered the establishment, I heard the unmistakable sounds of Jerry Vale's "Al Di La." I was puzzled and disconcerted. Was the presence of this music ironic? Was it a sign of a mordant sense of humor on the part of the staff? Or was there a specific, non-ironic reason this music was being played? Was this part of that continuing Baby Boomer–Gen X conspiracy to confer retroactive secular sainthood on hopeless second-stringers like Burt Bacharach, Dean Martin and Louis Prima? Or was it yet the latest confirmation that life is inherently random and ultimately meaningless?

After a few more numbers ("Sogni d'Oro," "Volare," "Te Adoro") I asked the twentysomething girl working behind the counter why she was playing Jerry Vale. She had no idea who Jerry Vale was. Then I asked the fiftysomething proprietor why Jerry Vale was being played and he had no idea either. Nobody in the establishment seemed to know how a Jerry Vale record had made its way into the compact disc player. Maybe somebody who worked the night shift had left it lying around.

Along with the CD containing such enduring classics as "Mambo Italiano."

The room was equally divided between Baby Boomers who had grown up despising Jerry Vale and his ilk, and Gen Xers who had grown up listening to the Thompson Twins and their ilk. None could possibly have had any cultural connection with Jerry Vale. Or his ilk. Until this point, I'd believed that at this late date in Western civilization Jerry Vale records could only be played for two reasons: because the listener actually liked them, or because someone was being *sassy*. Now I had a third explanation: The puckish, mega-snarky staff who worked the graveyard shift were leaving their satirical talismans lying around the shop where unsuspecting ingenue day shift employees would find them and absentmindedly stick them in the CD player, oblivious to their boundless satirical connotations.

Some may say I am making too much of this. Well, walk a mile in my shoes before reaching that decision. And listen to Jerry Vale while you're doing it. The problem is: I cannot stand being in an environment where unexplained ironic developments may be transpiring. I do not feel that I am alone in this view. If ABBA is playing in the background, I need to know why. If Bread's "Baby I'm-a Want You" can be heard off in the distance, I need an explanation. If David Cassidy, Christopher Cross or Kiki Dee is coming through the loudspeakers, there had better be a good reason.

And I don't feel that I need to say too much about my position regarding the Carpenters.

There is one other example of Gen X–Baby Boomer cultural miscegenation that warrants discussion: the transgenerational hipness check. Speaking in my capacity as a Baby Boomer, I am always distressed when I hear of fifty-year-olds who go out of their way to seek slacker approbation in a frantic search for acceptance. Is Keith still considered cool, they wonder. How about Neil Young? Will the Beatles now be dismissed as lightweights because Michael Stipe described their work as "elevator music"? Where does Gen X stand on Lou Reed and David Bowie? Where does folk music fit into all this? We Boomers basically agree now that folk music was a bad idea from the very beginning, but what do you youngsters think? Should we be buying some Dar Williams records? Lucy Kaplansky? Are the Indigo Girls now considered has-beens? And while we're on the subject, is it okay for us to say that Melissa Etheridge's music sucks now that she's broken up with Gabriella or Evita or Medusa or whatever her name is?

OF ALL THE intellectual and psychological congress that has transpired between Baby Boomers and Gen Xers there is nothing more disturbing than the concept of "Staff Recommendations." Encouraging the staff to make their own recommendations is a typical Baby Boomer ploy, a completely insincere gesture rooted in a spirit of preemptive condescension, a clever mechanism by which Boomer employers fleetingly *empower* the pouty, underpaid, going-nowhere-fast underlings they secretly despise.

Speaking as a person who has logged a few miles on the cultural odometer, I can't imagine anything lower on my list of Things to Do than to find out what the people earning the minimum wage at the local video store think I should be viewing these days. It's not just the predictability of their choices—invariably, it's going to be a Belgo-Manchurian animated film about a female vampire with AIDS, starring Shannon Tweed, Harry Dean Stanton and somebody who looks like Björk—just as the Staff Recommendation at the bookstore is invariably going to be a luminous novel written in incandescent prose by a Finnish dwarf child prodigy who was molested by a cross-dressing Cypriot brain surgeon while on her way to Graceland. No, it's not the predictability of it all that gets to me. It's the insolence.

Since when does anyone care what shop clerks think about anything? Who died and left them in charge? Are we suddenly going to have Staff Recommendations in gas stations? (*"We really think very highly of the Super Unleaded."*) Pizzerias? (*"The Staff thinks you should go with the calzone; the white pizza is shockingly substandard."*) Concert Halls? (*"We recommend the Moroccan Rai Festival; it would be foolish to waste your money on the Berlin Philharmonic."*) Or used-CD stores? (*"Why buy Pearl Jam when for the same price you can get Chin Huan-Kei: Empress of the Pipa?"*) Or churches? (*"We recommend that you confess to simony and sloth; murder and theft are just so tired."*)

I realize that in making these comments, I may have come perilously close to sounding like the Baby Boomer who thinks he knows everything. Far from it. I do not know, nor have I ever known, everything. Stephen Hawking knows everything. But I still know a hell of a lot more than the staff at any video store I've visited recently. So if you think I'm going to sit around and wait to hear what they have to say about my latest video rentals, well all I can say is: *As if. I don't think so. Hello!!!!*

Whatever.

8

Play That Funky
Music, White Boy

- -

Once upon a time there was a man called Che. Like Stalin, Hannibal, Attila and Sting, he was one of those epoch-straddling figures who required no last name to be identified. When I was coming of age in the 1960s, Che was viewed by a major segment of my generation as a hero, an incorruptible who ranked right up there with Albert Camus, Jean-Paul Sartre, Rudy the Red and Warren Beatty in the Pantheon of Phantasmagorically Together Superheroes. At the time, Che occupied the same hallowed inner sanctum as Patrice Lumumba, Frantz Fanon, Malcolm X, Angela Davis, Eldridge Cleaver and Eugene

McCarthy. As an icon of principled dissent, Che was Giuseppe Garibaldi, Emiliano Zapata, Leon Trotsky and Maximilien Robespierre all rolled into one. In large part this was because he had been shot, which was the only sure way to become a hero to Baby Boomers back then.

But much as we admired his revolutionary ardor and his commitment to the cause of agrarian communism, a great deal of Che's appeal had to do with his appearance. Not to put too fine a point on it, Che had *the look*. His thick, but not too thick, beard clicked with an entire generation, and with most major ethnic groups. His fiery Hispanic eyes, burning with third-world fury at first-world injustice and second-world mediocrity, drew rave reviews from both sides of the gender bend. But in the end, it was the beret that completed the package. Cocked on the side of his head in a style less influenced by canny French farmers than by psychotic French paratroopers, Che's beret seemed to scream: *"Check it out, bootlicking swine! I am packing! I am styling! I am the vicar of foreign affairs! Get in my face and we are going to take this thing outside. For I, Che, am ready to rumble."*

Today, more than thirty years later, it is hard to imagine what an immense stylistic influence Che exerted on young people at the time. Unlike Mao Tse-tung, who was fat and ugly and wore hideous gray suits, or Stokely Carmichael, who was skinny and bespectacled and wore kaleidoscopic dashikis that had little cultural resonance among white people, Che provided young men in my demographic group with a comfortable, accessible style of left-leaning haberdashery that was suitable for just about any occasion. Not until John Travolta popularized the urban cowboy look in the early 1980s would a swarthy young stud exert such a dramatic, far-reaching influence over young, contemporary male attire.

Unfortunately, berets went out of fashion in the late seventies, as did socialism, and because of the relatively inglorious circumstances of Che's demise (he was gunned down by the ultra-downscale Bolivian army while trying to spread the gospel of agrarian communism in the wrong neighborhood), he eventually retreated into the off-site storage unit of history, only occasionally reemerging as a figure of mirth, a target of derision, fodder for routines in Woody Allen movies, a self-parodying buffoon in one of the finest Monty Python routines ever. This is a roundabout way of saying that his shelf life was microscopic. Which is why today most people under the age of thirty-five have only the vaguest notion of who he was. If they even have that.

Navel-gazing Baby Boomers like to think that subsequent generations grow up learning not only about George Washington and Abraham Lincoln, but also about the pop cultural icons of the previous generation. Wrong, wrong, wrong. Gen Xers have no idea who Eldridge Cleaver and Angela Davis and Bobby Sherman are. They have never heard of Cinque What's-His-Name and the Symbionese Liberation Army. They wouldn't know Jean Shrimpton and Jane Asher if they came up and bit them on the ass. Not that they should. Nor that Jean or Jane ever would.

To Boomers, this is yet another shocking example of the vast lacunae in the formal education of their successors. Baby Boomers have a surprisingly hard time accepting the fact that every generation elects its own cultural heroes, and that these heroes are largely interchangeable. Baby Boomers always want to shove the heroes of their youth down everyone else's throat. So they keep playing the same records (by the time the average Baby Boomer reaches age sixty-five, he will have heard "Baba O'Reilly" and "We Are the Champions" 237,654 times), and they keep making the same invidious comparisons, and they keep sneering: "I knew Jeff Beck. I saw Jeff Beck. And sonny, Beck is no Jeff Beck."

OF COURSE, THIS is exactly the sort of thing Baby Boomers said they were not going to do. They promised not to put themselves on a pedestal.

They lied. A bright, shining example of their perfidy is the spanking-new Experience Music Project Museum in Seattle. This goopy, loopy, swoopy surrealistically pillow-like building—and the institution it houses—illustrates how Baby Boomers have deluded themselves into thinking that what once mattered to them should now matter to others. What's more, they have beguiled themselves into believing that what matters today will still matter tomorrow. And fifty years from tomorrow. This is a dicey proposition at best.

Viewed holistically, the EMP amalgamates the salient characteristics of the Boomer generation: a fixation on their own reflection, not to mention the reflection of their own reflection; a determination, however futile, to institutionalize the evanescent; and a fatal misconception that if you build a museum to house a collection of objects, the objects, by some process of cultural alchemy, will become transubstantiated into objets d'art.

This sort of lunacy did not start in Seattle. It started in Cleveland, with the 1995 erection of the Rock and Roll Hall of Fame. On the surface, it would seem that this museum was an underhanded attempt to confer an institutional legitimacy on a genre that had not yet earned it in the marketplace of art. By this I mean that, while Monteverdi's *L'Orfeo* has already lasted four hundred years, I strongly suspect that the Turtles' "Happy Together" will not. Nor, for that matter, will "Honky Tonk Women," "Love Me Do" or "Billy Jean." This is no reflection on the Rolling Stones, the Beatles or Michael Jackson (though it is definitely a reflection on the Turtles). It is a reflection of the facts. Pop music, because it is so much a product of its era, has a hard time surviving that era. It is of a time and place, but times change and places vanish. Frank Sinatra's music has had a longer shelf life than Dean Martin's and will certainly have a longer shelf life than Ricky Martin's. But in time it too will fade away. Its pertinence then contains the seeds of its obsolescence now. This is the Faustian bargain that all musicians accept when they decide to compose "For Your Love" rather than "Für Elise." No wonder Billy Joel is so hard at work on *An American in Sag Harbor*, or whatever it is that he is "composing" out there on Long Island.

Viewed more generously, the Rock and Roll Hall of Fame is a relatively benign institution. Though it focuses primarily upon music associated with Baby Boomers, it also pays homage to trailblazers such as Johnny Cash and to more recent, non–Baby Boomer, generally deserving acts such as the Plasmatics and Guns n' Roses. It's also worth bearing in mind that the driving force behind the Hall of Fame was never artistic but commercial; Cleveland wanted the museum because it hoped it would increase tourism. The Rock and Roll Hall of Fame is silly, but it is not stupid. And, within the parameters of a severely circumscribed and generally unambitious musical genre, it does have a relatively wide scope.

A very different sort of museum is Seattle's EMP. The brainchild of Paul Allen, cofounder of Microsoft, the fourth wealthiest man in America and the very embodiment of the Rock 'n' Roll Plutocrat, it was designed by the wildly fashionable architect Frank Gehry, who also designed the Solomon Guggenheim Museum/fun palace in Bilbao, Spain. It cost $240 million to build, which will get you a pretty nice rock 'n' roll museum, but wouldn't even cover the down payment on an art museum. Previous generations of plutocrats would have made sure that Seattle had a world-class museum of art, which it does not, before erecting a temple to ephemeral pop culture. But Baby Boomers are cut from a different cloth. Besides, van Goghs are pricey.

The most amazing thing about the Experience Music Project is that it is not immediately apparent what it is a museum *of*. The Metropolitan Museum of New York is a museum of great art. The Museum of Modern Art is a museum of modern art. The Carole and Barry Kaye Museum of Miniatures is a museum of miniatures. But the

Experience Music Project is essentially a Museum of What Personally Matters to the Baby Boomer Who Built the Damn Thing.

Originally, the museum was intended as some sort of municipal *homage à Jimi Hendrix de Seattle,* Allen having apparently decided that the single most influential musician in the history of rock 'n' roll had not yet received his due. This is why he incorporated the code word "Experience"—as in "the Jimi Hendrix Experience" or "Are You Experienced?"—into the official curatorial nomenclature. Nudge, nudge. Wink, wink.

Obviously, with the passage of time, the allusive symbolism of the word "experience" will recede and then vanish. It may already have done so; my fourteen-year-old son barely knows who Jimi Hendrix is, and certainly couldn't pick the names Noel Redding and Mitch Mitchell—Hendrix's minimally talented sidemen—out of a linguistic police lineup. Is Allen aware of any of this? I doubt it. The way he sees it, if the word "experience" meant something to Baby Boomers, then it must mean the same thing to everybody. Isn't that why we were put on this great planet?

In any case, the day I turn up, I enter the museum with extremely subdued expectations. They will soon subside further. After anteing up the absurd $19.95 entrance fee and toiling through a snap tutorial in which I learn how to operate the elaborate handheld computer that serves as one's guide in "contextualizing" the gestalt of the art form quasi-immortalized by the institution, it soon becomes apparent that Hendrix's music, films, guitars et al. are not the only focal point of the institution. The museum is dedicated to rock 'n' roll in general. Or so it seems. But where then are Keith Richards's syringes, Rod Stewart's scarves, John Bonham's shot glasses, Elton John's mammoth sunglasses? Ah yes, as I continue my pilgrimage, it gradually becomes clear that it is a museum devoted to *American* rock 'n' roll.

But no, in time-honored Baby Boomer fashion, the focus proves to be even more nuanced, layered and generally complicated than that. As I stagger into one of the main exhibit areas, clutching the contextualizing guide, I find myself inspecting exhibits such as:

Jacket, circa 1965, worn on Stage by Phil "Fang" Volk of Paul Revere & the Raiders.

Japanese SG copy, electric guitar, circa late 1970s, used by Kurt Bloch of the Cheaters.

Coat, circa 1980s, worn by Nancy Wilson of Heart.

Obviously, I do not react to these exhibits the way I would were I inspecting the pajamas Mozart died in or the smoking jacket Beethoven wore when he composed *Fidelio*. For that matter, it's not even like seeing the brandy snifter Dean Martin sipped from when he recorded "That Little Old Winemaker, Me." As usual, it's a case of much ado about nothing, with Baby Boomers not only opting for quantity over quality, but hoping that quantity will actually be mistaken for quality.

Yet in one sense the displays are immensely informative, for they enable us to see Baby Boomers at their most maddeningly self-absorbed and detail-oriented. First, the previously noted obsession with disseminating minutely detailed information about something that is not terribly important, thus fulfilling British historian A. J. P. Taylor's fear that as the documenting and archiving arts become more specialized, people will end up learning more and more about less and less. Second, the use of nebulous, *faux-recherché* terms such as "circa" to create the impression that Kurt Bloch of the Cheaters was such a mysterious, elusive figure that the precise dates when he incinerated the fingerboard of his bottom-of-the-line guitar cannot be determined. Third, the curator's fusion of the edifyingly persnickety and the completely half-assed. *"We know that Kurt Bloch—whoever the hell he was—used this guitar sometime, but we're too goddamned lazy to go out and find out when. Like what, did you expect us to carbon-date it?"*

One thing that concerns me is the nettlesome question of authenticity. In one corner stands a jacket from the 1980s that was supposedly worn by Geoff Tate of Queensryche. Over there sits an electric guitar that, local legend has it, was used for the cover of a Metal Church album in 1984. But how do we know that the jacket allegedly worn by Geoff Tate of Queensryche did not in fact belong to Greg Sage of the seminal Seattle punk/garage band the Wipers? How do we know that the Japanese SG copy, electric guitar, circa late 1970s, supposedly used by Kurt Bloch of the Cheaters, did not actually belong to Andrew Wood of Malfunkshun? Or Damon Titus of the Enemy? Or for that matter, to Phil "Fang" Volk of Paul Revere & the Raiders? Are there rock antiquarians who specialize in cataloging this sort of arcane memorabilia? Or did the Experience Music Project staff simply stuff this junk in the display cases because they figured: *Who's going to run out and check?*

As I continue through the museum, frantically pump-
ing the computer for more contextualization about Nancy
Wilson at the time she allegedly wore that circa 1980
jacket, I happen upon numerous display cases containing
tantalyzing bits of information such as this:

*When the Viceroys guitarist Jim Valley joined Portland's
Don & the Goodtunes, he brought along the gem "Little
Sally Tease," which became a classic Northwest radio hit
in 1965.*

and

*For a period in the 1960s, the Raiders were about the
biggest rock band in America.*

This is complete hogwash. Paul Revere & the Raiders
may have had a few hits in the mid-sixties, but if they were
the biggest rock band in America, it must have been during
the fifteen minutes that Brian Wilson was visiting his therapist. Hey, I was there. But this is beside the point. For as I
inch past the exhibit of hypnotically uninteresting items
that once belonged to such putatively pivotal Seattle-based
punk bands as the Wipers, the Tupperwares, the Lewd, the
Telepaths and the Fartz, the truth suddenly hits me like a
ton of bricks. I had entered this oddball museum assuming
that it was an institution essentially dedicated to talking
about my generation. But no, it's much more narrow-band
than that. It's a museum largely devoted to talking about
my Pacific Northwest Generation. It's a cross between the
Rock and Roll Hall of Fame in Cleveland and the Science

Museum anywhere. It's the Seattle/Tacoma/Portland/ Bellingham/Spokane/Walla Walla and Points West Rock and Roll Hall of Fame. It's as if Philadelphia—which can effortlessly lay claim to more enduring rock 'n' roll history than Seattle, Tacoma, Portland, Walla Walla, Spokane, Bellingham and Cleveland combined—had built a self-referential rock 'n' roll museum with such exhibits as:

Doo Rag, circa 1965, worn on stage by Kenny Gamble of the Soul Survivors.

or

Trousers, circa 1960, once twisted in by Chubby Checker.

There's contextualizing for you.

Don't get me wrong. I admire Aberdeen's homegrown Nirvana. I thoroughly enjoy the Seattle-based Pearl Jam. I think it's nice that the Ventures came from Tacoma, that Paul Revere & the Raiders started in Idaho, that the Kingsmen hail from Portland. Heck, I think it's terrific that Elvis came from Tupelo. But what's that got to do with anything? Everybody has to be somewhere. Everybody has to be *from* somewhere. Some bands are from Seattle and some are from Atlanta and some are from Los Angeles and the best band of them all is from Liverpool. Is there a point I am missing here? Why are Baby Boomers continually startled that famous people grew up locally? Christ, even Jesus grew up somewhere. And as for these interminable exhibits of the Wipers and the Tupperwares and the Fartz, well, frankly, Mr. Allen, *who cares?*

In the final analysis, Paul Allen's Experience Music Project is a series of micro-museums of what is personally important to a select group of Baby Boomers. *"Here's a load of crap associated with third-tier Pacific Northwest bands I used to listen to when I was growing up. I really liked them; they meant a lot to me; I hope you enjoy them."* It's a bit like opening a Museum of Black Leather Vests. Here's my vest, circa 1975. Here's my vest ten years later. Here are my friends' vests, circa 1976. And here are some vintage vests that belonged to some guys from Tacoma back in the 1960s. God, did we look cool in our vests. Don't forget to check our great gift shop, so you can do the most ridiculous thing of all in post–Baby Boomer America, which is to buy pointless memorabilia in a museum devoted to pointless memorabilia.

Yet let us be fair to Paul Allen and his dubious venture. It does contain a series of karaoke-type recording rooms where visitors can form their own bands with friends, family or complete strangers, record their own songs, and perform them in an environment that attempts to simulate the excitement of a real, live rock 'n' roll show. Wowie-zowie. It also showcases an amusement park "ride" called "Funk Blast: The Artist's Journey," where visitors can vicariously experience the world of seventies funk and find out how James Brown, Chaka Khan and the Funkadelics created their unique sound. Ugh. This "attraction" underscores the age-old truth that middle-aged white people always develop a guilty affection for whatever young black people were doing thirty years earlier, while reviling whatever young black people are doing today.

The museum also features a room where visitors can

vicariously (and belatedly) participate in the Jimi Hendrix "experience." Here, it's hard not to wonder what Hendrix, whose art, whose personality, whose outlandish attire, whose entire career were all about breaking the rules and turning the world on its ear, would make of a sleek, sterile, family-oriented Brave New Suit museum whose walls are covered with bizarre, pedagogical, old-fogey messages such as:

Nothing is as exciting as a live dance, party or concert.

I think Paul Allen may have had help from Bill Gates on that one.

As I stagger toward the exit, I stop long enough to inspect the museum's impressive collection of guitars: some old, some new, some unusual, some actually played by famous people. None of it registers. I'm reminded of the time I inspected Paul Simon's handwritten lyrics for "Sounds of Silence" in Cleveland's Rock and Roll Museum and felt absolutely nothing. It wasn't like you were looking at the Magna Carta or the Shroud of Turin or the wine bill from the Last Supper. Or, for that matter, Chopin's favorite piano. Guitars are so common and of such recent provenance that it is almost impossible to be impressed by them. I personally own six guitars and I cannot even read music. Half the men in America have de facto guitar museums in their bedrooms. Standing in that room I don't feel much different than I would have if I had visited a Museum of Quite Fascinating Trees. For the Experience Music Project to knock you back on its heels, it would need the vomit that Hendrix choked on, or Kurt Cobain's last hypoderm. It would need a display of girdles and fanny firmers and liposuction machines that once belonged to Ann Wilson. It would need something irreverent and noninstructive and real. It would need something straight from the heart of rock 'n' roll.

THE EXPERIENCE MUSIC Project is a radiant symbol of Baby Boomer self-absorption. Everything we touch gets turned into a commodity. Since we don't have any battlefields we want to talk about, we have commodified our adolescence. Lacking an Iwo Jima or a Bataan Death March, we have commodified Woodstock, Altamont, Haight-Ashbury, Monterey.

And to what purpose? Every generation has great popular music. But it is only great to those who think it is great. No matter how tenaciously people try to hang on to it, the music rarely survives, because each new generation at some point makes the healthy decision to reject, and usually deplore, the music of its parents. By mistaking the heroes of one's youth for the heroes of everyone's youth, by producing piles of baubles and trinkets and data and dodgy memorabilia in an effort to immortalize what is inherently transitory, we try to gain access to history through the back door. Baby Boomers have never come to terms with the fact that the past is not stagnant, that it keeps expanding to include younger people's pasts. Younger people are going to have a finite amount of interest in the guitar that was once used on the cover of the 1984 Metal Church album. They'll be too busy building their own museums of hip-hop, their own cultural mausoleums stuffed to the gills with shoes that once belonged to Kid Rock, with guns that were once fired by Puff Daddy. Or if things get really esoteric, guitars once played by They Might Be Giants.

All that said, the Experience Music Project is not without a certain historical value. Baby Boomers are well known for their End of Days mentality, always rattling on about the last picture show and the last man standing and the last action hero and the last of the brave and the end of history: They are intoxicated by hyperbolic millennialism, by the all-consuming belief that after us comes the deluge, when in fact after us will simply come more stuff. A deluge *did* come after Louis XV, but it's highly unlikely that it's coming after "Louie Louie."

If future generations want to know precisely how narcissistic and self-adulating Baby Boomers were, they need only drop by Seattle for an afternoon. There they can visit a garish, ludicrous monument that a New Age Ozymandias built to himself. Look on my works, ye mighty, and despair. Look on a jacket that once was worn by Eddy Vedder and despair. Look on a guitar pick, circa late 1980s, once used by Kurt Cobain before he met Courtney Love, and despair. Look on a jacket once owned by Phil "Fang" Volk of Paul Revere & the Raiders and despair.

I've despaired already.

9

American History:
The B-Sides

W hile demanding unquestioned fealty to their own gods and goddesses, Baby Boomers have long manifested a shocking contempt for the heroes of previous eras. Throughout their first half-century on the planet, Baby Boomers have repeatedly hauled famous historical figures into the court of public opinion and subjected them to merciless revisionist caterwauling for their alleged crimes against the people.

As touched upon briefly in an earlier chapter, this tendency reflects the discomfort Baby Boomers have always felt for the actual past, and explains why they are constantly revising, reconfiguring and reupholstering history, desperately attempting to shoehorn the facts into a more soothing, politically correct framework. Accordingly, Columbus must be castigated, Washington calumnied, Jefferson demystified and Davy Crockett ridiculed, while villains like Aaron Burr or primordials like Geronimo are recast in a more compassionate light.

This affection for "alternative" versions of history is also part and parcel of the Boomer obsession with alternative versions of anything: alternative film takes (now available on DVD), alternative album cuts, alternative album covers, alternative rookie baseball cards, even "alternative" rock, as if rock 'n' roll as an art form were vast enough to contain quantifiable alternatives. Responding to this Boomer mind-set, I have devised a brief alternative history of the United States, told as things might have turned out had Baby Boomer values flowered at an earlier point in our national adventure.

WITH THE WORDS *"Que pasa?"* on his lips, marine biologist Christopher Columbus clambers out of the waves at Samana Cay on October 12, 1492, and is greeted by a throng of congenial aborigines who are obviously living in a vast tropical paradise. Columbus's expedition across uncharted waters has been financed by reverse CMOs arranged by the Kingdom of Castille; the hapless investors forced to settle for a slice of the third tranche are still grumbling about the PIKs and Chinese paper that got shoved down their throats. Initially, Columbus plans to claim the New World for King Ferdinand and Queen Isabella. But when he sees that the inhabitants of the island are living in an equatorial Utopia with no disease, no crime, no prejudice and no peer pressure, and also realizes that an invasion of new microbes from the Old World would wreak havoc on their pristine ecosystem, he turns around and returns to Spain, never breathing a word about his discovery.

For the next hundred years, the New World remains shrouded in mystery. Then, in 1592, an English fishing boat runs aground near Roanoke, Virginia. The survivors establish a thriving colony, with tobacco as their primary cash crop. The product becomes hugely popular in England. But when researchers at the Royal Academy of Science in London discover that tobacco contains noxious substances that could lead to cancer, heart disease, asthma and birth defects, the Crown formally bans its sale. With its economic underpinnings stripped away, the Roanoke colony collapses.

In 1619, French explorers reach the site of what is now Montreal and establish a thriving fur-trading operation with the Algonquin tribe. They also build North America's first restaurant, Même Pas. But after an initial flurry of interest back home, French couturiers come down hard on the fur trade, contending that it is cruel to animals. Wealthy Parisian courtesans are more than happy to clothe themselves in recycled gunnysacks. The colony collapses.

Two years later, the French return and establish a thriving lumber operation. But when the Indians point out that cutting down the woodlands of the primeval Eastern forest could have a disastrous effect on the North American ecosystem and lead to the annihilation of such species as the tawny egret and the great northern otter, the French pack up and go home.

In 1627, the first successful European colony on the shores of North America is finally established, when a party of 102 English men, women and children seeking refuge from religious persecution in the Old World land at Plymouth, Massachusetts, which they rename Montebello Close. That winter is the most severe in four hundred years, and it is highly doubtful that the Pilgrims could have survived without generous help from the Wampanoag tribe, whose leader, Hits the Ground Running, sends a massive supply of maize, gourds, apples and freshly killed free-range ducklings to the outpost. "Thanks for sharing," say the settlers, "but next time could you bring some kiwis, pomegranates, smoked salmon, cognac, chestnuts, fresh arugula, porcini mushrooms, Provençal *brugnons*, oven-roasted tomatoes and passion fruit?"

Three years later, the first successful French colonies are established, one at the mouth of the Mississippi, one at the mouth of the Saint Lawrence and one at the mouth of the Missouri. They are called Nouvelle Orléans, Nouveau Beaujolais and Nouveau Riche. In English America, a permanent colony in Virginia is established in 1645 by entrepreneurs who turn marijuana into a cash crop. Because the harvesting, processing and marketing of marijuana is extremely labor-intensive, the entrepreneurs consider importing slaves from Africa. But religious leaders persuade the planters that slavery is morally wrong. So the planters invite 400,000 Africans to come work in the fields, identifying them on immigration forms as "nannies."

Initially, relations between the settlers and the Indians in the various colonies are quite good. The Pequots introduce the Pilgrims to the concept of the sweat lodge, where they can energetically beat on tom-toms and weep and blame their fathers for everything bad that ever happened to them. The Pilgrims teach the Indians how to turn butternut squash into penne and use dried bark coloring to simulate squid-ink vermicelli. But by the middle of the seventeenth century, Indian chieftains are becoming concerned that their people are adopting the white man's customs at the expense of their own. Edgy young bucks are often seen wearing black hats and buckled shoes and saying things like "Goodie Squanto, raise thy game a level." Others have begun playing air banjo. And a number of braves have drifted off to Boston to appear in the popular Pilgrim cabaret revue, *Great White Father Knows Best*.

Finally, in April 1656, full-scale war erupts. First, Hiawatha drowns during an infant swimming class under Niagara Falls. Then word gets out that unscrupulous traders have been selling the Indians blankets contaminated with herpes and Epstein-Barr virus. The French join the Indians in the war against the English-speaking settlers. As will become their custom, they lose.

Many colonists fight in the war, and many lose their

lives. But many more decide to stay home. Those who do not take up arms against the Indians are conflicted by their failure to join the army. In 1687, twenty years after the war, a famous journalist publishes an essay in *Towne and Countree* in which he expresses regret for not having fought in the French and Epstein-Barr War. Opposed to the conflict on moral grounds at the time, he now fears that he missed out on a wonderful bonding experience by not doing his military service.

FIFTY YEARS AFTER the first permanent colonies were established in North America, the New World still has little in the way of entertainment. Then one morning in April 1683, a Salem, Massachusetts, woman named Anne Hutchinson announces that she is a witch and has had regular sexual congress with Satan, Moloch, Baal and Beelzebub. Shortly thereafter, a vivacious governess named Tituba reveals that she has had similar experiences with a succubus named Courtney, the first instance of satanic lesbian possession in American history. The pair hook up and open a popular eatery called Seasonings of the Witch in what is now Nyack, New York, which attracts visitors from all over the East Coast.

Meanwhile, relations with the Indians continue to deteriorate. In July 1695, Dignity Taylor, a one-legged Mennonite, attempts to jog from the Atlantic to the Pacific to raise public awareness about the plight of one-legged Mennonites. A few miles outside New Ritalin, he is captured, flayed, parboiled and eaten in a *fricassée légère* by the Shawnee in a rite henceforth known as Burning White

Man. Seemingly, the Shawnee are furious that the colonists' homeopathic approach to treating smallpox has not worked. A savage war erupts, and once again the French and Indians are badly beaten.

As in the past, many colonists are deeply conflicted about the war against the Shawnee. One highly respected journalist publishes an essay in *Common Sense* in which he expresses regret for not having fought in the war. Opposed to the conflict on moral grounds at the time, he now fears that he missed out on something important by not doing his military service, that it would have been a great bonding experience.

By the early 1700s, people all across the land have begun to yearn for an earlier, simpler time before the New World lost its innocence. Up and down the Eastern Seaboard, portly, middle-aged men gather on weekends to reenact famous battles. Particularly popular are the Second Punic War, the Battle of Thermopylae, the St. Bartholomew's Day Massacre and the War of the Roses, which takes three days to perform in its entirety. A small group of men even stage reenactments of the French and Epstein-Barr War.

Meanwhile, the Indians have fallen on hard times. Fearing that they are losing market share to the more charismatic Sioux and Apache tribes, the Algonquins and Hurons change their names to the Montreal Heat and the Toronto Sting in 1734. Their archenemies, the Iroquois, shorten their name to the Fightin' Quois. Meanwhile, the Pawnee and the Shawnee merge, citing a similar product name and obvious synergies. The Ute and the Paiute soon follow suit, and the Cherokee rename the Trail of Tears *La*

Strada Lacrimosa, hoping to attract a better class of settler. Increasingly, colonists are sending their young men to live with the Indians as boarders, in the hope that the hardscrabble aborigines will whip the boys into shape. In exchange, the Indians send their children east to train as conflict-resolution specialists and out-placement counselors for displaced tribes like the Cree, the Delaware and the Mohican.

In Boston, New York and Philadelphia, colonists are beginning to chafe under British rule. Incensed by the high taxes on beverages, a gang of men disguise themselves as Indians in May 1774 and dump the contents of two ships into the harbor. Shortly after the Boston Chai Tea Party, in protest against the Crown's medieval stance against abortion, Minuteperson Betsy Ross appears naked and pregnant on the cover of Benjamin Franklin's *Poor Richard's Almanac*.

The next year, war breaks out. In April 1775, firebrand patriot Paul Revere conducts his famous midnight ride to Concord and Lexington, bellowing, "Concord and Lexington; we have a problem." In July 1776, Nathan Hale mouths the immortal words "I only regret that I have but one lifestyle to give for my country." In December of that year, Captain John Paul Jones, his own ship the *Bonhomme Richard* irreparably damaged, is warned to surrender by the commander of the British frigate *Serapis*.

"In your face," replies Jones.

As is always the case, the public is of two minds about the conflict. In August 1781, three days after the British surrender at Yorktown, a right-wing journalist publishes an essay in *Burr's Content Provider* in which he expresses regret for not having fought in the Revolutionary War. Opposed to the conflict on moral grounds at the time, he now fears that he missed out on a positive bonding experience by avoiding his military service.

THE FOREIGN OPPRESSOR thrown off, colonials are soon at each other's throats. In 1802, Jefferson is impeached by his enemies in Congress, who accuse him of having slept with a slave named Sally Hemmings. "It depends on what you mean by *slept*," says Jefferson, who is narrowly acquitted. In 1803, Jefferson dispatches Meriwether Lewis and William Clark to explore the massive interior of North America. "I'm all over it," says Lewis.

Lewis and Clark hire the type A Shoshone princess Sacajawea as a guide. But because Sacajawea is pregnant, the expedition is ceaselessly delayed by her overladen Conestoga wagon, filled with flash cards, strollers, suntan lotion, manuals, organic baby food and music boxes playing snatches of Mozart that constantly scare the buffalo away. Sacajawea is eventually murdered by a Nez Percé squaw who gets tired of all the canceled play dates, and the expedition turns back. Oregon is never discovered.

After Jefferson's term expires, the nation enters a period known as the Era of Good Vibes. In December 1805, James and Dolley Madison give birth to a daughter named Madison, who will eventually found a magazine called *Avenue*. Many years later *Avenue* will spark a huge journalistic controversy when it asks the dreaded Apache warrior Geronimo to be guest editor. In a story entitled "My Pony Soldier, My Rapist," Geronimo will explain that the reason he mistreated so many women throughout his career was that he had been sexually abused by Kit Carson as a child.

Meanwhile, the country is changing in many ways. In 1819, onerous taxes on imported liquor lead to the Blended Whiskey Rebellion, followed the next year by the Pinot Grigio Rebellion and subsequently by the tragic Cabernet Sauvignon Rebellion of 1823. In 1825, James Fenimore Cooper publishes a semi-autobiographical novel in which one of the characters is Andrew Jackson's penis. No one complains. Around the same time, a rural Ohio couple name their son William Tecumseh Sherman in honor of the dreaded but respected Shawnee warrior. Duly impressed, numerous Indian tribes begin using white people's middle names: Crazy Jason Horse, Sitting Jared Bull, Black Jenna Kettle and Dances with Britney's Wolves.

In June 1835, 183 Texas freedom fighters led by Colonel William Travis, Jim Bowie and Davy Crockett take refuge in a deserted Spanish church in San Antonio, Texas. They are surrounded by an army of five thousand Mexicans under the command of the hyper general Santa Anna. Santa Anna gives the Texans one hour to surrender, telling them it would be a sign of hubris to decline. Travis unsheathes his saber and draws a line in the sand.

"Those who wish to stay and fight, step over this line," he says. "And those who think we have no business being here—big-picture types who see that we are merely the craven representatives of an odious, imperialist, racist nation and are engaged in a completely immoral, totally unjustifiable war against a hapless third-world country—feel free to leave now."

All 183 Texans leave, including Travis himself.

Out west, tensions continue to rise. In November 1844, the artist Albert Bierstadt receives permission to wrap the entire Great Plains in a gigantic pink cloth. But stampeding buffalo, possibly provoked by the Kiowa, rip the artwork to pieces. The same year, the Santee open a fantasy camp where white men can accompany aging warriors in an actual raiding party against the Creeks. But harsh feelings between the white man and the red man are more the norm: Furious at the Comanche for raping and murdering everything that moves and for abducting scores of latchkey farm children and then refusing to attend sensitivity training classes to learn aggression management techniques, three thousand college women launch a Take Back the Night campaign along the Rio Grande. They are raped and murdered.

Back east, the tragic conflict that will pit brother against brother, father against son, and third nephew against stepcousin twice removed is about to begin. In the rural south, inspired by the classic *Uncle Tom's Cabana*, underpaid nannies seeking to escape from oppressive conditions begin using the Underground Railroad in 1851. Two years later, the federal government closes the Underground Railroad, citing recurring safety violations. In April 1861, the Civil War breaks out, but the news does not immediately reach certain parts of rural America. On May 11, 1861, Jeb Stuart happens upon two hundred oddly dressed men carrying crucifixes, miters, censers and pitchforks. He massacres them. A lone survivor informs him that the men were Albigensian Crusade reenactment buffs acting out the apocalyptic siege of Montsegur, which took place in 1244. Stuart refuses to apologize to the widows, sneering, "No pain, no gain."

The war does not go well for the South. Stymied in his efforts to attract overseas investors, Jefferson Davis hires a British advertising agency to "reposition the Confederacy." The agency proposes emancipating its 4.5 million "nannies" and redesignating them as "gardeners," "security personnel" and "hospice companions." The agency also recommends that the Confederate Army change its drab colors from gray to black-and-teal.

In April 1863, Abraham Lincoln deals the South a crushing blow when he redesignates all five million nannies as "messengers." Six months later, speaking without notes, Lincoln makes his famous Gettysburg Statement:

My sense of it is: the battle is kind of a mixed bag. Clearly, the Confederacy and the Union were not on the same page, yet even though 51,000 men got waxed, I view this as a win-win situation because everyone showed grace under pressure despite casualties up the wazoo, and Gettysburg will now be the benchmark against which all future battles are judged.

Speaking for the entire Lincoln family, I'd like to congratulate the Confederacy for taking things to another level. So could you all put your hands together and give it up for Mister Robert E. Lee and the Army of Northern Virginia? Personally, I think that we have all learned a lot from this as a people and that the experience will only make us stronger. We will go forward, rather than backward. We will put this thing behind us. We now realize that a starter house divided against itself cannot stand.

Finally, I'm happy that the battle didn't end in a draw, because at least after Pickett's Charge we have closure.

In April 1865, a few weeks before the war ends, Lincoln is assassinated at Washington's Ford's Theater during a performance of *Our American Cousin, Cousine.* Plunging from Lincoln's private box onto the stage, the actor John Wilkes Booth exclaims, "*Sic venti latte,*" the state motto of Vermont.

Once again, many young men are forced to reconsider their attitude toward the war. Twelve minutes after Lee surrenders at Appomattox, a famous writer publishes an essay in which he expresses regret for not having fought in it. Opposed to the conflict on moral grounds at the time, he now fears that he missed out on something very important by ducking his military service, because it would have been a good bonding experience.

WITH THE WAR over, the government can finally resolve the Indian situation once and for all. Oddly, as the century is drawing to a close, Native Americans have become hugely fashionable. The public gobbles up books like *Ute Without Tears, Arapaho in 30 Days, Oglala for Nitwits, Bury My Heart at Hyperextended Knee* and *Mescalero Kids Say the Darndest Things!* X-treme scalping comes into vogue in New York, where a state-funded university comes under fire for a seminar in which a therapist stakes out a man on an ant hill, presenting the ritual as a legitimate form of foreplay. Things get completely out of control when a noted opera singer is found scalped in his hotel room. Was he trying to kill himself? Was he murdered? Or was this another case of autoeroticism that went awry?

But in the end, the friction that has characterized relations between the white man and the Indians will lead to tragedy. In June 1876, Colonel George Armstrong Custer arrives at the Sioux and Cheyenne village on the Rosebud River in Montana. "Don't go there," he is warned by his scouts, but he ignores them. Custer informs the celebrated medicine person Sitting Bull that peace pipes are now illegal in teepees containing room for fewer than 125 people.

The next day, Custer and his entire command are wiped out in the most devastating defeat ever suffered by the United States Cavalry. Custer's last words are, "You guys rock!" Forty-eight hours later, a journalist asks President Ulysses S. Grant: "Taking the long view, do you feel that the Sioux were trying to send a message with their slash-and-burn, take-no-prisoners approach?" Grant retorts: "Hey, when the Hunkpapa Sioux sneeze, the whole frontier gets a cold."

After the massacre, the Indians flee north to Canada,

which is celebrating the new Canadian-American holiday, Cwanza. Crazy Horse is now plagued by recurring nightmares. In these dreams, the entire Sioux nation is exterminated by armies of pony soldiers as numerous as grains of wheat, and he himself is impaled on a bayonet wielded by an Indian policeman who has betrayed his own people. Crazy Horse eventually consults with a reservation Indian who has studied feng-shui at a missionary school in Encino, and is told to shift the location of his tent so that the entrance flap points west instead of north, to pitch his tent within earshot of a babbling brook, and to deep-six all those scalps, because their presence is allowing enormous amounts of negative *chi* to seep into his teepee.

Meanwhile, social mores are changing fast. In May 1883, confirming rumors that have been circulating for years, Annie Oakley and Lizzie Borden reveal that they are live-in lovers. In a subsequent interview with *Calamity Jane* magazine, they announce plans to raise a child fathered by Wild Bill Hickcock, Billy the Kid, Jesse James, Wyatt Earp, Deadeye Dick, Bat Masterson, Pat Garrett or "whoever happens to be available that night."

In May 1886, at halftime of the Buffalo Bill Wild West Show in Boston, the now retired Sitting Bull marches to the center of the ring and apologizes for annihilating the Seventh Cavalry and mutilating their bodies. "Clearly, mistakes were made," he concedes. "But we want to get past that."

Seconds later, Custer's widow, Libby, comes out of the stands and agrees to accept a kiss and a hug from Sitting Bull.

The next day, a conservative journalist publishes an

essay in which he expresses regret for not having fought at the Little Bighorn. Opposed to the conflict on moral grounds at the time, he now fears that he missed out on something very important by not doing his military service, regretting what would have been a good bonding experience.

As the frontier era draws to a close, Americans long for bygone days before the nation lost its innocence. In his book *The High Green Chaparral*, the Winnebago shaman Thanks You for Being There laments the destruction of the "prairie cathedrals" of his youth. White men are similarly nostalgic for the past. One very popular traveling show called *Behind the Musket* features Civil War veterans talking about their misspent youth.

"We had the whole ball of wax: fame, money, horses, guns, women," says General Longstreet. "But then personal rivalries tore the Confederacy apart. Bobby wanted to carry the war to the north. The Jebmeister got involved with his wife's magazine, *Martha Stuart Living*. Everybody liked Jeff Davis, but he kept bringing his wife, Varina, around and she was just a bitch on wagon wheels. Then one day I had to deliver the saddest piece of news ever: Stonewall had been shot dead. After that the whole thing fell apart. We had a few laughs at Gettysburg, but by Bull Run II we all knew the Confederacy was unraveling. We tried to get people back on message with that Ku Klux Klan reunion in 1895, but things were never the same. There was just too much bad blood. The healing never began. In the end, I think we all realized that the journey is at least as important as the destination. But now the journey is over. All things must pass. All things must fade away."

Adds the aging, sickly General Beauregard: "In a very real sense, those were the days, my friend. We had zero tolerance for the idea that they'd ever end. We were deeply committed to the notion of singing and dancing forever and a day. We were totally into the concept of choosing the lifestyle we'd choose, pushing the envelope so that we would fight and never lose. For when the shit came down we were young and sure to have our day."

10

Good Lovin' Gone Bad

But what about the more recent past? How might history have unfolded had the original values and attitudes associated with Baby Boomers taken root? Every so often, I try to visualize how much better life could have turned out if Baby Boomers had stuck to their idealistic guns and not turned into middle-aged zombies who spend their free time comparison shopping for apricot-ginger spice cake with rum glaze and Bistro lentil soup, while preparing Algerian lamb shanks with cardamom and orange (for best results, use one-half cup of blanched slivered almonds, two large fennel bulbs and perhaps just a pinch of saffron; and to really impress guests, prepare a fresh leek salad on the side, bathed in a delicate vinaigrette). Moreover, what would life be like if they had not turned into middlebrow scum?

Well, for starters, Americans would have rejected America and said no to Yes. Billy Joel would be working as an A&R guy for the Lawrence Welk Orchestra down in Branson. *Cats* would have bombed twenty years ago, without ever reaching New Haven. Loggins & Messina would have opened a storefront law office, right next to Seals & Croft, directly across from Emerson, Lake & Palmer, a few yards down the hall from the famous ambulance chasers Chapin, Chapin, Manilow and John. The man responsible for manufacturing the terms "No way, José," "wiggle room," and "What rocks your world?" would have been killed in a car accident in San Jose, coincidentally colliding with the woman who invented the terms "cocooning," "networking" and "mentoring." When their obituaries appeared in the newspapers the next day, no one would call either of them a "poster child" who had survived a "hardscrabble" childhood, nor would anyone suggest that they died because of excessive "hubris." No, it would be a straight car-crash story.

Also, there would be no Van Damme films.

If the fabulous idealism of the 1960s had prevailed, this society would be a very different place. By the middle of Jerry Brown's second term, all social injustice would have been eliminated. Private schools would have ceased to exist. Peace, love and understanding would have swept away the gun lobby. Minorities would be incredibly prosperous and happy, which would eliminate the need for brooding, mean-spirited rap music. The absence of rap music would make middle-aged white people feel incredibly happy, as would all that state-subsidized Colombian Gold authorized by FDA chief Timothy Leary and his assistant, Chong. And housing would be much less expensive because sensitive landlords would gladly hold down rents in an effort to build a bridge to the underclass.

Desirable as these developments might be, it is a mistake to think that this nation would necessarily be a better place simply because the Age of Aquarius had come to pass. Sadly, many less attractive facets of sixties culture would now cast a long, dark shadow over the present. For one, everyone would be living in charmless communes with no bathroom doors. Two, everyone would be driving microscopic electric cars that could only travel forty miles without being recharged. Three, there would be a ridiculous amount of public nudity, which was fine when women were young and nubile, but which could be kind of unpleasant now. Four, all men capable of growing a ponytail would have grown a ponytail, including Alan Greenspan. Five, bands like Poco and New Riders of the Purple Sage would be performing at presidential inaugurations, with Buffy Sainte-Marie and Leonard Cohen reading lengthy passages from Richard Brautigan's *Trout Fishing in America*. Six, because of orgies and group sex, children would have no way of ever finding out who their real parents were, which would cheat them out of one of the crowning moments in life when the young adult confronts his parents with evidence of their myriad crimes, publicly blames them for everything unpleasant that ever happened to him and declares, in a voice loud enough to be heard by the neighbors, "I never asked to be born." And seven, there would be a genuinely alarming amount of middle-aged belly dancing.

In fact, none of these things have come to pass, because Baby Boomers did abandon the lifestyle and values of their youth and turned into the god-awful people that they are. Yet here again we are faced with a troubling paradox, for bad as Baby Boomers are, they could have been worse. In fact, I believe they could have been *much* worse if they'd really put their minds to it.

Reflect carefully before dismissing this extravagant hypothesis out of hand. Suppose everyone *had* taken it to the limit one more time? Suppose consciousness *had* been raised? Suppose everyone *had* loved the one they were with in the absence of the one they loved? Suppose everyone in this society *had* let it all hang out? Or even part of it? Finally, what kind of a society would this be if everyone *had* Wang-Chunged tonight?

I know that contiguous and noncontiguous generations both older and younger have a hard time visualizing how Baby Boomers could possibly be more odious than they already are. It is like trying to imagine even *stronger* grappa. As they silently fume in the dark corners of the gigantic dance hall that some call America, watching portly Baby Boomers waddle across the floor in an obscene parody of the Hustle, or drag their spoiled, sullen insufferable children to their very first Crosby, Stills, Nash & Young show, or remind everyone for the four-thousandth time where they were when those three civil rights workers got pulped in Philadelphia, Mississippi, it is difficult for other generations to imagine that Baby Boomers could possibly take up any more space than they already do. And yet, the honest truth is: The world handcrafted by repugnant Baby Boomers could have been a whole lot worse. Imagine the following horrifying time line:

- 1964. Styx appears on the *Ed Sullivan Show* for eight weeks running. This helps a severely traumatized country recover from the unexpected assassination of President Richard Nixon.
- 1965. Billy Joel's career starts eight years earlier.
- 1966. Peter Fonda, not Dennis Hopper, gets the real career, replacing Sean Connery as James Bond in *Ulee's Goldfinger*.
- 1967. Al Stewart replaces Brian Jones in the Rolling Stones. The group immediately disbands after "Year of the Cat" and "Time Passages (Are on My Side)" fail to set the world on fire.
- 1968. Peter Fonda wins the Oscar for Best Actor for his role in *Ted and Alice, Bob and Ulee*.
- 1969. Styx's "Come Sail Away" sells 36.7 million copies the day it is released.
- 1970. Jim Morrison does not die. Neither does Janis Joplin or Jimi Hendrix or Duane Allman.

Instead, each appears on a duets album with Mel Torme entitled *The Velvet Fog Trips Out*.

- 1971. Jim Croce's plane lands safely.
- 1972. So does John Denver's.
- 1973. Styx breaks up because the rhythm guitarist keeps bringing Yoko Ono to the studio. An entire generation is devastated.
- 1974. Ben & Jerry invent premium ice cream, debuting with the flavors Chicago Farrago, Papa John Peach and Santana Banana.
- 1975. Cat Stevens releases a duets album with Frank Sinatra entitled *The Teaser and the Firecat Meet the Chairman of the Board*. Then, when it is already too late, he becomes a Muslim.
- 1976. ABBA does the sound track for *Apocalypse Now*. The film, in which Anson Williams plays a troubled Green Beret sent into the jungles of Southeast Asia to assassinate an insane Marine colonel played by Robby Benson, is the biggest-grossing film of all time.
- 1977. Jerry Brown begins serving his second term.
- 1978. Word gets out that there is more than one Dan Fogelberg.
- 1979. Marvin Gaye, Chaka Khan, the Funkadelics and Gil Scott-Heron appear on the Tull tribute album.
- 1980. Mark David Chapman empties a revolver at the Captain and Tenille, ELO, Judas Priest and the Bee Gees, but misses.

- 1981. *Billy Jack VII* wins the Academy Award for Best Picture.
- 1982. Frank Zappa records "Love and Marriage" with Frank Sinatra on *Duets, Volume III*. Iggy Pop is featured on "Softly As I Leave You," Ravi Shankar on "The Lady Is a Tramp."
- 1983. Cher opens a chain of theme restaurants where all the waiters look like Sonny and all the waitresses look like Chastity.
- 1984. Billy Joel records *Piano Men* with his long-lost twin brother, Joel.
- 1985. *Toto XXXVIII* is released.
- 1986. Cher, not Sonny, gets elected to Congress.
- 1987. Peter Fonda, Bridget Fonda and Jane Fonda star in *My Dinner with Ulee*. It narrowly edges *The Rose VI, Grand Canyon IV* and *The Big Chill III: This Time It's Personal* for Best Picture.
- 1988. Nobel Peace Prize winner Jimmy Carter's face replaces Teddy Roosevelt's on Mount Rushmore.
- 1989. The Doors set up the first Rock 'n' Roll Fantasy Camp. Jim Morrison demonstrates how to expose oneself onstage without getting arrested. Ozzy Osbourne shows how to tear a live pigeon's head off. Duane Allman explains defensive driving techniques.
- 1990. Peter Fonda and Susan Sarandon star in *Thelma and Ulee*.
- 1991. Following protracted negotiations with Mark Farner to join a dramatically reconfig-

ured Grand Funk Railroad, Jim Morrison decides to join the Traveling Wilburys.

- 1992. Debbie Boone, Billy Ocean, Leo Sayer, Spyro Gyro, Bonnie Tyler, Bread, Air Supply, Andy Gibb, Debbie Gibson, Journey, Kiki Dee, Rick Springfield, Blue Cheer, Helen Reddy, Olivia Newton-John, Uriah Heep, Kansas, Blue Oyster Cult, the Cowsills, Bette Midler, David Soul, Vangelis, Nazareth and Suzi Quatro are inducted into the Rock and Roll Hall of Fame. At the induction ceremony, Jimi Hendrix sings "Baby I'm-a Want You" with Bob Dylan, Mick Jagger, George Harrison and the Average White Band.
- 1993. Geraldo Rivera replaces Ted Koppel on *Nightline.*
- 1994. Jim Morrison records *Faith and Begorrah: 'Tis the Celebration of the Lizard* with the Chieftains.
- 1995. Janis Joplin, Barry Manilow, Alice Cooper, John Denver and Placido Domingo record the entire *Ring* cycle on a double *Duets* album with Barbra Streisand and the long-dead Mario Lanza.
- 1996. The United States Constitution is altered, allowing Michael Dukakis to serve an unprecedented fourth term.
- 1997. *Grumpy Old Easy Riders*, starring Peter Fonda and Dennis Hopper, is released to rave reviews.
- 1998. *Moondance! The All-Singin', All-Dancin'*

Life and Times of Van Morrison is a gigantic hit on Broadway.

- 1999. Uh-oh. It turns out that Ali McGraw didn't die at the end of *Love Story*. After Ryan O'Neal stormed out of the hospital, the doctors detected a weak heartbeat and have kept her cryogenically frozen for almost thirty years. Now Jenny and her Mozart Köchel listings are back!
- 2000. Robin Williams is elected to the United States Senate.

11

Aging Disgracefully

- -

Much of this book has been devoted to reproaching Baby Boomers for their selfishness, their self-adulation, their fascination with the inner child who died a long, long time ago, and who did not die a natural death. Now I ask myself if I have inadvertently neglected, or at the very least slighted, the more compelling issue of my generation's fundamental ridiculousness. After all, Baby Boomers now occupy most of the important political, economic and cultural positions in this society, and represent this great nation on the world stage. Yet for the most part,

with their dysfunctional refusal to grow up and their con-
comitant inability to get a fashion clue, the entire generation is embarrassing themselves, their children, their
parents, the whole country.

I do not say this out of a sense of resentment, disappoint-
ment or, God forbid, hatred. Far from it. If anything, I am
prepared to extend the olive branch to a generation that has
done nothing to deserve it. More specifically, I am offering
the benefit of my advice. For as our journey draws to an
end, and as our circle becomes closed, I sense that it is time
for the healing to begin. It is high time that we Baby
Boomers, as a generation, finally get our act together and
recognize that this really *is* the first day of the rest of our
lives, and start acting accordingly. To facilitate this, I have
devised a multifaceted program whereby Baby Boomers
can atone for their numerous crimes and salvage something
from the complete mess they have made of this society.

Let us review the situation carefully. Early in their lives,
Baby Boomers backed themselves into a corner from which
they could never extricate themselves. That is, *they never
devised an exit strategy from their youth*. They never figured
out how to age gracefully. In fact, they never figured out
how to age at all. Since all Baby Boomer culture is concerned with maintaining an aura of coolness long after this
is appropriate, or even possible, Baby Boomers now find
themselves lost at sea. And as is so often the case with
Baby Boomers, now that they find themselves lost at sea,
they also find that they have not brought the right clothing.

A generation ago, late-middle-aged men who had
fought at Monte Cassino and Corregidor inexplicably
began wearing fuchsia-colored polyester pants with white

patent-leather shoes and matching white belts and lime green jackets, while their middle-aged wives dressed in a style best described as Early Hospital Employee: billowing slacks, flowery tops, malignantly functional shifts. They looked preposterous, but that was okay, because that was their look and they stuck with it. Conversely, their children wore bell-bottoms and tie-dyed T-shirts, which also looked absurd, but this was also okay, because that was their look and they stuck with it. It didn't matter if everybody dressed in a clownish fashion, as long as everybody dressed in a clownish fashion that was congruent with the accepted standards of their generation. In other words, as long as everybody stayed in the box.

Now consider contemporary attire. Seditious to the end, Boomers have refused to accept the intergenerational sartorial covenant that had worked so well for more than two hundred years. Instead, Baby Boomers now want to dress like slackers, with oversize shorts and ironic polyester shirts and magenta-and-lime sneakers and spray-painted toreador pants that display the demure tattoos poised at the summit of their porcine glutes. They wear their baseball caps in every which direction; they wear clothes that are too bright and tight and flashy for them, and worse, they wear clothes associated with a generation that despises them, and which they despise in turn. This makes no sense; it is like Jews dressing up as Cossacks; like *campesinos* decking themselves out to resemble death squads. It only confuses the issue.

Baby Boomers have misspent their valuable middle years by failing to lay the groundwork for old age. Middle-aged people in previous societies gradually recognized that the main objective of human life was not to be wealthy or wise or influential or even happy, but simply to get off the planet with as much of one's dignity intact as possible. You didn't want to be beheaded or roasted on a spit. You didn't want to be eaten by cannibals. You didn't want to be garroted by a scarf that got caught in the wheels of your car. Much less your scooter.

Because Baby Boomers have spent so much of their lives either being young, wishing they were still young, trying to recapture their lost youth or pretending that they are still young, they have not put the proper emotional distance between their births and their deaths. They could have learned about this by reading a few good books; instead they read Peter Mayle and Tom Clancy. From Aristophanes to Plautus to Molière to *The Blue Angel,* literature and films are bursting with heartfelt entreaties to fiftyish men to accept that their youth has faded and to stop making fools of themselves. This is a roundabout way of saying that fifty-seven-year-old men should not still be wearing PINK FLOYD: SET THE CONTROLS FOR THE HEART OF THE SUN T-shirts.

In order to restore the dignity we once possessed as young people, it is going to be necessary for Baby Boomers to go back and address some of these vexing issues. Boomers need to make smooth the path that has become crooked. As a generation we must not only atone for the crimes we have visited on our countrymen, but also make restitution. Baby Boomers are going to be around for another thirty to forty years, and it's vital that we take steps to ensure that the other generations can get along with us during the difficult times ahead. Here are a number of useful suggestions I would like to see implemented at the earliest possible opportunity.

Massively reduce the videotaping. It's nice that you have all those tapes of Jedediah's first step and Maya's first pre-school molecular biology camp, but now that the kids have some age on them, we probably won't be needing footage from Dorian's first trip to a socialist republic or Seth's first protest against inequitable oil depletion allowances. Look at it this way: We don't have a videotape of Thomas Jefferson writing the Declaration of Independence, so we can probably do without Alex's first aikido class.

Support taxpayer-funded pensions for rock stars. Every week, the tabloids carry at least one heartrending story about a former heavyweight champion or NBA all-star who is now living in a rat-infested drainage ditch under the Santa Monica Freeway. Frankly, I don't see how that's any worse than Marty Balin and the Jefferson Starship being forced to sing "Revolution" in front of 286 subdued Boomers in a cavernous old theater in Tarrytown, New York, on a frigid February evening; at least the athletes in the drainage ditch don't have to mortify themselves. And they don't have to travel.

But that's beside the point. Baby Boomers are always complaining about how depressing it is to see the idols of their youth dragging themselves around into their dotage. If Baby Boomers are so upset by the spectacle of their heroes reduced to wandering-troubadour status, they should agree to have a portion of their income taxes go to support aging rock stars so that they can come in from the cold. If Baby Boomers are not willing to put their money where their mouths are, then they're just going to have to grin and bear it when another of these rambling wrecks comes to town.

Stop ragging on Mick. Baby Boomers are masters of Machiavellian emotional distancing techniques, one of which is to ridicule pathetic old rock stars for refusing to act their age. Admittedly, Mick's sashaying his ancient hips while rasping through "Satisfaction" is a troubling sight. But Baby Boomers themselves don't think they look ridiculous doing their annual Disco Inferno routine at the high school fund-raiser or hoisting their rheumatoid jumpers every Saturday morning or holding up their disposable lighters at Madison Square Garden as the Who gamely hack their way through "Teenage Wasteland" for the one-billionth time. Mick may look gnarled, emaciated, addled. But at least he doesn't have a forty-eight-inch waist.

Establish a Federal Witness Relocation Program for guitarists who were once in John Mayall's Bluesbreakers, who *do* have forty-eight-inch waists. This may just be a personal thing, but the once willowy Jimmy Page, Mick Taylor and Peter Green are all absolute porkers these days. Couldn't we all pitch in some money to get these guys both out of mind and out of sight? They owe it to us. We owe it to them.

Inaugurate T-Shirt Amnesty Day. Once a year, the federal government should declare a twenty-four-hour amnesty during which aging hipsters can turn in their Grateful Dead, Jethro Tull and Black Sabbath T-shirts without fear of reprisal. Quite often, people who own these shirts can't bring themselves to burn them, fearing a symbolic incineration of their youth. But many others worry that their grandchildren or third wives may one day happen upon these telltale costumes concealed in the attic T-shirt Museum and demand an explanation, the way septuagenerian Germans are sometimes summoned front and center by their progeny to explain those suspiciously natty Gestapo uniforms.

In taking possession of these incriminating articles of clothing, the government must promise to bury them in secret underwater landfills, lest they be shipped to third world countries and one day reappear as the uniforms of irony-minded Marxist insurgents. This would be particularly true of those Dexys Midnight Runners roadie jackets. And anything involving Frampton.

Absolutely no fashion statements after the age of fifty. Baby Boomers erroneously assume that fashion statements are made via flashy new clothing. In reality, fashion statements are made via flashy new flesh. Thin young girls look good in anything. Thin young guys look good in anything. Old, fat guys look bad in some clothes; even worse in others. Consider the tank top issue. Tank tops were designed for mobsters and for young men who do not yet have muscles, but who one day may. Tank tops were never designed for middle-aged men, and particularly not for those with a lot of gray hair protruding from their burly chests and hairy underarms. Earrings are also a terrible idea; what are you, Long John Silver? *"You want an eyepatch and a parrot to go with that, sir?"* Another thing: Get rid of the *Sticky Fingers* T-shirts. We know you once saw the Rolling Stones. We know you were once a rebel, perhaps even a rebel, rebel, you old diamond dog, you. What would surprise us would be if you didn't wear a *Sticky Fingers* T-shirt and weren't once a rebel. For an idea of how ridiculous you have become, imagine what a Deion Sanders–style doo rag would look like on a senior citizen. Then imagine what it would look like on you. Guess what. You *are* a senior citizen.

Deep-six the secular mythology. Every time a Baby Boomer takes his son to a baseball game, he acts as if this is the seminal bonding event that his son will still be talking about when he is ninety. This is another case where Baby Boomers insist on having something and its opposite. On the one hand, they want to act like baseball stadiums are postmodern cathedrals where mythological events regularly transpire. On the other hand, they know that baseball players are avaricious scum. Let's bring René Descartes into the discussion for a second. If baseball players are scum, then it follows that the stadiums they play in cannot be truly sacred places. They are stadiums and nothing more. And kids don't buy into this crap anyway. That Field of Dreams, Boys of Summer hooey might work at Yankees Stadium or Wrigley Field. But how are you going to sell that yarn to a kid who grew up rooting for the Padres? Frankly, I think the reason so many young boys go in for wrestling is because it is a direct, healthy, *sane* reaction to their fathers' green-cathedral loopiness.

Stop stirring the echoes of Gettysburg. Baby Boomers seek to atone for not going to Vietnam by making semi-annual pilgrimages to Gettysburg, usually with a child named Cole in tow. Then they come back and talk about man's inhumanity to man, the senselessness of it all, the vanity of human wishes, and how much fun it was to bond with Cole at the site of Pickett's Charge. I went to Gettysburg with my son and we visited the site of Pickett's Charge, and we both came away with the same impression: *What were those Johnny Rebs thinking of?*

In short, the whole Civil War buff thing is beyond me, one Baby Boomer crime for which I will not take the rap. Not long ago, I read a *New York Times* piece written by a guy who took his son to Gettysburg and decided that it was absolutely swell. In it, the reporter theorized that the lingering appeal of Gettysburg might be that no one actually knows why so many young men came to that idyllic locale on a brutally hot July morning to kill one another. This is not true. The Confederates came to Gettysburg because it was another one of Robert E. Lee's terrible ideas, and the Union soldiers came to Gettysburg to make sure he realized it. The logic underlying the Battle of Gettysburg isn't hard to decipher: Them dumb crackers got whupped.

And while we're on the subject, could we please knock off the reenactments? The day I visited Gettysburg, there were literal phalanxes of middle-aged men wearing shirts identifying themselves as veterans of various battles fought by the Army of Northern Virginia. In other words, these jokers seemed to have gotten it into their heads that being a veteran of a Civil War reenactment was the same as being a veteran of El Alamein or the Bataan Death March or Tet. *Fellas, could I have a word with you in my office?*

Rethink the dancing issue. While it is inadvisable for white people to dance in the best of times, there should be official government strictures against any white person dancing past the age of forty. That includes Madonna. More than any other human activity, middle-aged dancing not only proves that the Fountain of Youth has run dry, but often makes it clear that the Fountain was never much more than a trickle in the best of times. A friend of mine who works for a major magazine says that there is nothing she dreads more than after-hours company events where alcohol is served, because the senior editors spontaneously start doing what she refers to as "the middle-aged white guy dance." The middle-aged white guy dance at its most pernicious is a St. Vitus–type spasmodic gesticulating derived indirectly from Baryshnikov and quite directly from Barbarino. A big corporate function with dancing invariably looks like the annual John Travolta Epileptic Impersonators mixer. For those requiring additional guidance in this troubling area, I recommend procuring a videotape of the *Seinfeld* episode where Elaine makes a fool of herself doing that spastic dance and everybody laughs. Don't laugh. It's you.

Stop celebrating victories you're not responsible for. Baby Boomers always act like they personally were responsible for ending lynchings in the South and bringing down Richard Nixon. The Freedom Riders ended the lynchings in the South. Woodward and Bernstein and Ellsberg brought down Nixon. The rest of us had nothing to do with it.

Keep your powder dry. Baby Boomers confront some hapless, asthmatic, emaciated old gin monkey puffing on a waterlogged Pall Mall in the no-smoking section of a deserted restaurant and act like they've just personally won the Battle of Britain. Or they shriek at some octogenarian tart for wearing a tatty old mink stole until she breaks down in tears, and then act like they're Pope Leo I confronting Attila the Hun at the gates of Rome. Since Baby Boomers are animated by such a strong sense of moral outrage, I suggest they stop squandering their resources on such defenseless targets and take aim at the big game. Suggestions? The next time you see a carload of teenagers blasting a song about raping your mother while gunning down a Korean grocer, read them the riot act. Upbraid them for their plangent philistinism. Lambaste them for their insensitivity toward women. Take them to task for their vulgarity. Once you're done with them, please go after the cell-phone-wielding drug dealer who's annoying everyone else on the subway, the pack of cretins defiling the art museum promenade with their skateboards, and the twelve rednecks with the Confederate flag draped across the back of the pickup truck. And if any of these punks try smoking in a public place, making sexist remarks or wearing fur, *really let them have it.*

Ditch those overalls. That's right, honey, we're talking about you. Maybe that You'll-Never-Guess-How-Big-a-Butt-I-Have-When-I'm-Wearing-These-Things look worked back in the Days of Rage. But these are the Days of Road Rage. Honestly, my fellow Americans, can't the federal government do something about this?

That goes for those black leather vests as well. What's bad for the goose isn't any better for the gander.

Start shopping for a casket. You're going to die just like everybody else died, and after you're gone life will go on. Get used to it.

Stop sharing your feelings. Americans, as a people, used to be very reluctant to share their feelings. Then along came the Baby Boomers with their hugs and kisses and I-love-you-man's. For thirty years it has been deemed culturally commendable to share one's innermost feelings about love, hate, childhood trauma, sexual abuse, parental alcoholism and even deviant behavior with everyone, everywhere, whether they want to hear it or not. Now it is time to stop. People like Suzanne Somers who triumph over immense personal problems love to write books telling the public that it is possible to overcome childhood traumas and become a wonderful person. No, it isn't. You still end up being Suzanne Somers. If you start out as an emotionally scarred human being and then engage in a four-decade program of self-improvement through self-expression, the best you can do is to become more like Oprah. Frankly, I don't think the game is worth the candle. My advice? Be like the people who founded this great nation. Be like the English. It's not just a question of concealing your emotions. Don't even bother to have any.

Stop blaming the schools for your dumb-ass kids. Affluent, forward-thinking, multiculturally sensitive Boomers watch their spawnlings struggle through their first six years of school, then get upset because the kids don't seem to be anything special. So, abruptly, they yank them out of public school and send them to de facto segregated private institutions that are expected to unleash their hidden talents. Folks, it's time to lighten up. The reason Gwyneth hasn't set the world on fire by the time she's twelve is because she's as thick as a brick. Better change her name to Marsha or Vanna, so that expectations will be lower when she gets to Albany State.

Abandon the quest for retroactive hipness. Smug thirtysomething rock critics, who themselves are fast approaching their cultural expiration dates, love to attend concerts given by dinosaurs and tee off on the geriatric crowds frantically trying to recapture the glory of their youth. Those crowds only exist in critics' addled minds. At an April 2000 Crosby, Stills, Nash & Young concert at Madison Square Garden and at a Who farewell concert later that year, I was struck by the fact that the crowd *did not* consist of dilapidated Boomers who had first seen the bands at Woodstock. The crowd instead was equally divided between those legions of amiable but dumb young people who, for God knows what reason, always seem to turn up at concerts at which they are demographically extraneous, and Boomers who were old enough to have been at Woodstock, but who obviously weren't. Half of them looked like narcs, the others like firemen. With their scars and mullets and chains and leather jackets, they looked like the thugs you see at a mid-December Jets-Bills game.

I would be willing to bet that 50 percent of the Boomers attending CSN&Y and Who concerts today actually served in the ROTC or the Green Berets back in the Summer of Love. And the other half are mobsters. Their belated attendance at CSN&Y or Who concerts represents a last-ditch attempt to lay claim to a hipness they could never lay claim to when they were young. They are the kinds of middle-American Baby Boomers who were always six inches behind the generational hair curve: wearing crew cuts when everyone else was wearing their hair like Cochise; growing Allman Brothers facial hair when everyone else was going with the James Bond look; still sculpting that short-on-the-top, long-in-the-back relief-pitcher hair when everyone else was taking their cues from Tom Cruise; subjecting their skulls to full-immersion Grecian formula rinses when everyone else had gone fashionably gray. In the end, I suppose, there is something sweet and innocent about this Rip van Winklish stab at being cool. Nevertheless, it is pitiful.

One of the most chilling offshoots of this search for retroactive hipness is a phenomenon known as the Postponed Ponytail. (I am aware that I go on about this subject more than is strictly necessary, yet I honestly believe that the clear-and-present menace posed by ludicrous locks cannot be overestimated.) The Postponed Ponytail is the sort of massive, garish, attention-getting weapon brandished by affluent middle-aged men whose autumnal prosperity allows them to evince a tonsorial flippancy they almost certainly did not evince in their youth.

Once, while standing outside Studio 54 at the intermission of *Cabaret*, I watched two ancient mariners emerging from the theater, each sporting a menacing ponytail. The taller man, in his late forties, had his huge locks spliced into two pigtails, making him look like a cross-dressing Goliath. The second man, well into his fifties, had his streaming gray hair done up Belushi-style, in a full-fledged samurai. Not surprisingly, the men looked horribly corporate, and quite astonishingly evil. I listened in on their conversation as they tried to chat with two elegant young Japanese women who were clearly not interested in going to dinner with men who looked like a fugitive Tweedledum and Tweedledee from an Outer Mongolian production of *Alice in Wonderland*.

All the while, I kept studying their faces, trying to visualize what they looked like when they were younger men, when the taller man was the head of the local SDS chapter and the shorter one ran the campus coffeehouse and had once jammed with Jerry Jeff Walker before he became famous. But I could not place their faces with the era. That's when I realized that this pair of follic parvenus had waited until they were rich enough to jump into the game. The taller man was obviously named Larry and was an entertainment lawyer. The shorter man was also named Larry and ran a very successful folding-chair rental company out in Syosset. They'd waited until the coast was clear in 1995, and then decided to fulfill their childhood dream of forming the Ponytail Posse.

I blame David Carradine for a lot of this stuff.

Fear not the Republican within. Baby Boomers grew up believing that Republicans were greedy, self-absorbed people with breathtakingly bad taste in clothes and music, and who weren't really comfortable around minorities. Today, that describes just about everyone in my age group. So let's stop acting like Republicans are beastly nomads fresh in from the steppes who seek to lay waste to our most cherished values. The truth is, voting Democratic past the age of forty is a silly affectation. We have met the enemy, and it is us.

Get off the stage. One of the things that Baby Boomers hated about their parents' generation was the refusal of moldy icons like Bob Hope and Bing Crosby to hit the showers. Our attitude back then was: You had your day in the sun; your day in the sun lasted a lot longer than it should have; now get thee hence. But Baby Boomers have done exactly the same thing. Keith refuses to go quietly. Cher still thinks she's hot. John McEnroe has challenged the Williams sisters to a tennis match. Honestly, is this any way for impending retirees to behave?

If you have to wear a baseball cap, please wear it correctly. I'm surprised that I even have to mention this. Middle-aged men who wear baseball caps turned backward do not look like Puff Daddy. They look like De Niro's doomed moron catcher in *Bang the Drum Slowly*. There are some things that middle-aged white people excel at. Fashion isn't one of them.

Be man enough to admit your mistakes. ELO, ELP, EST, ESP, ESL, Jimmy Carter, amateur photography, Jill Clayburgh movies, drugs, Vietnam, confiscatory tax rates, breast implants, divorce, Mike Dukakis, transcendental meditation, the Promise Keepers, personal trainers, intuitive healing, test-tube babies, surrogate mothers, Hanoi Jane, decks, waterbeds, nanny cameras, self-hypnosis, most forms of woodworking, *A Brief History of Time*, Geraldine Ferraro, the men's movement, jogging at lunchtime, primal therapy, *Kraftwerk*, cowboy hats, facial hair, sensitivity training, "Free Bird," Montana, peasant dresses, Earth Shoes, leftist ice-cream companies, multitasking, George McGovern. Come clean. Fess up. Move on.

Stop playing the belated ethnic card. There is a certain kind of Baby Boomer who is always rediscovering his forgotten Tejano or Blackfoot roots. Baby Boomers who are

1/256 Choctaw are always springing this little micro-tidbit in the middle of dinner as if it were a concealed derringer. "True, your ancestors may have been brought here as slaves," they seem to intimate, "but my people had their land stolen right out from under them. . . ." *Well, I guess your full house beats my three queens.*

Let's establish statutes of limitations on everything. How about a bar code expiration date beyond which "Benny & the Jets," "A Horse with No Name," "The Dock of the Bay (Sittin' On)," "Peaceful, Easy Feeling" and anything by the Four Tops can no longer be played? Or a statute of limitations on the entire Kennedy family? Shouldn't there be term limits on people named Fonda? And don't we also need a National Nepotism Monitoring Act, stipulating that no more than one child of a famous person can go into the same field as their parents? Between the Charlie Sheens and the Patrick Kennedys and the Jeb Bushes, haven't we all suffered enough? As a famous man once said, what do you have to pay to avoid going through all these things twice? Bob should know; he's Jakob's father.

Take a walk on the wild side, you old fart. Honestly, is it absolutely necessary for every single person in this society to be reading exactly the same book at exactly the same moment? Couldn't one Baby Boomer come out and admit that he hasn't read *The Killer Angels* and doesn't give a damn if he ever does? Couldn't one wishy-washy, PBS tote bag lady with a cat named Perseus come out and admit that *La Vita è Bella* is sentimental crap? Does everyone always have to be reading *Angela's Ashes*, *A Thousand Acres*, *All the Pretty Horses*, *Midnight in the Garden of Good and Evil*? Couldn't one goddamn person over the age of forty read a Ngaio Marsh mystery for a change?

If you suddenly drop everything to move to Vermont and become a potter, don't act like you've made the world a better place. How many pots and Portuguese pressed-glass tumblers does one society need, anyway?

Fuck Vermont. I've been wanting to say that my entire life.

Never trust anyone over thirty. The Baby Boomers have made extra sure that this continues to be extraordinarily good advice.

Stop acting like you're the first person to ever turn fifty.

Movement tootsies, return to your homes. You know who I'm talking about. You come out of the woodwork every four years in your insouciant berets and continent-length scarves, brandishing your dog-eared copies of *The Bell Jar* every time some geriatric crypto-lefty runs for public office. So long ago and far away they touched your perfect body with their minds, but that was yesterday, and yesterday's gone. Besides, isn't there some better use to which your talents could be put? No bromeliads that need watering? No lathes to be cleaned? No haiku chapbooks that cry out for your adroit calligraphic stylings?

Make up your mind about Vietnam. One way or the other.

Make peace with your Maker. This is extremely important advice, because when the Last Judgment arrives you can be sure that God is going to remember every last one of your slurs and slights, your calumnies, your insults, your witticisms, your blasphemies, your bons mots, your general cattiness. You may not be terribly comfortable with the term "God," preferring "Higher Power" or "Prime Mover" or "Life Force." But God Himself prefers the term "God"—it works for Him—and if you have dissed Him or gotten in His face in any way, He will gird His loins, gather His raiment about Him and take your sorry ass down. Remember: Just because you don't believe in God doesn't mean He doesn't believe in you.

Last but not least, get a grip. Listen up, guys and gals. Take it down a notch or two. Mellow out. Put the cell phone away. Stow the laptop. Get off the mountain bike. Shelve the goddamn video camera. For once in your life, just go with the flow. Stop being so manic. Stop being so neurotic. Stop being so . . . *so*. Remember: *Other people have to live on this planet.*

A PERSONAL NOTE: Now approaching fifty myself, I do not feel it is too late for Baby Boomers to recapture some of the idealism of our youth, to reassert ourselves as the crusaders we were in the sixties, to perhaps move up a few notches in the generational rankings. In other words, to reinvent ourselves, which is the one thing Baby Boomers have always done better than anyone else—*ever*. But in order to achieve this, we have an awful lot of work to do. We have to stop the incessant navel-gazing. We have to reacquire a sense of personal dignity. Most important of all, we have to stop talking about ourselves. And we have to stop talking about ourselves not for just an hour, not for just a day, not for just a year, but always.

I'm going first.

12

Stop Me If You've
Heard This One

Now that I think about it, I *do* have a few more things to say before I go. A friend of mine once remarked that when Baby Boomers are old and decrepit, no one is going to go out and make a *Saving Private Ryan* commemorating their finest hour. They didn't have a finest hour; they only got their fifteen minutes of fame. Anyway, no young person watching a Baby Boomer tearjerker—*Saving Ryan's Private Placement*, for example—would come away feeling teary-eyed or awed. Boomers do not inspire those kinds of emotions. They are resourceful and smart, but they are not notably courageous and they certainly are not lovable.

The Baby Boomers are not the worst generation, and, if history is any guide, many far worse generations will come after them. Someday, troubled young men seeking inspiration from antiquity may even gather together on Saturdays to engage in reenactments of late-twentieth-century warfare. Because there are no Boomer military triumphs worth simulating, they will be forced to reenact scenes from corporate warfare such as the takeover of RJR Nabisco or Time Warner's merger with AOL. Just as Civil War reenactment buffs carp and cavil over authenticity, some insisting that real Confederate soldiers would not have worn shoes, corporate reenactment buffs will argue over the importance of wearing yellow ties and red suspenders or, in the case of Bill Gates, drab sweaters. They will engage in bitter shouting matches, jockeying over who gets to play Steve Jobs as he strides into a combative customer's boardroom and seethes: "Either you take this goddamn operating system as is, bugs and all, or we walk." Not exactly McAuliffe at Bastogne sneering "Nuts!" to the Germans. But it's a start.

Before we conclude, two questions need to be asked. First, do Baby Boomers know how awful they are? Of course not; that's the whole point of being self-absorbed: No pertinent information ever seeps in from the outside. The entire generation is hermetically sealed from reality, not unlike Sammy Davis, Jr., Howard Cosell and Czar Nicolas II, who seemingly had no idea how much everybody else hated them.

Second, will things ever come full-circle, to the point where Baby Boomers will be viewed with affection, however grudging, by their children? The answer to this question is also, I believe, no. Let me explain why.

Every spring I take my mother to a dance at a local community college, where the music is provided by one of the ghost bands from the thirties. Some years it is the Tommy Dorsey Big Band, sometimes Glenn Miller; one year the Artie Shaw Orchestra showed up. My mother, now eighty, still loves to cut a rug. As I whirl her around the dance floor, any animosity I may have felt toward her generation when I was a young man fades away. This is partly because her generation no longer holds any real power, but it is also partly because hers was a generation that finally grew up. As the last strains of "Stardust" linger in the background, I am struck by how thoroughly lovely Agnes Catherine McNulty, child of Irish immigrants, Depression survivor, working mother of four, now looks in the late autumn of her life.

But I doubt that the children of Boomers will ever feel that way about their parents. For one, we really *do* dance like Elaine on that *Seinfeld* episode. As we grow older we will almost certainly not grow wiser; we will simply think of new ways to be preposterous. And our children will resent us for that. They will know that our moment has passed, but they will also know that we will never accept this. Our dotage will provide no illumination, no cure for a half-century of self-delusion. Then, as now, we will perceive ourselves as the crown of creation. But unlike Thomas Jefferson and John Adams, falling into each other's arms shortly before their deaths on July 4, 1826, astounded at all they accomplished as young men, we will still be listening to "Teenage Wasteland" and "Revolution." We may even be listening without irony. As humans age, hearing is the first faculty to atrophy, then vision, and then one's keenly developed sense of humor, honed over a lifetime of interminable smarminess.

I am not so far removed from my youth that I cannot remember what it felt like to be a young person growing up in America in the 1960s. Behind all the discord and madness, there was a sense that ours were worthy, noble dreams, that great things lay ahead of us, that we were going to make our mark. Most important of all, there was a sense, now half-forgotten or cynically mocked, that we were all in this thing together. But then we got fat and lazy and smug and self-indulgent and quite spectacularly dull. We started waxing nostalgic about our youth before our youth was even over; we started taking moral shortcuts; we set our dreams to the side, and by the age of forty we'd had it. We never had another moment of passion or daring after we stopped taking drugs.

We were good at making money, but in the end, it was the only thing we were really good at. Sadly, we could never enjoy the money as much as other generations could, because we were the generation that insisted that it wasn't going to opt out. But we did. We got co-opted. We got suckered. We did get fooled again. And again. And again. Our fate eerily paralleled Paul's: We started out as the Beatles; we ended up as Wings.

We were prodigiously clever, but shallow. We feared large themes and deep thoughts, and it showed in our music, our literature, our art and most of all in our facile journalism. We mistook big for important, complex for profound, clever for powerful, pop culture for culture, lifestyle for life. We could not stick to anything. We flitted. We discarded one bad idea after another, just like Tom and Daisy. In the end, the best book ever written about Baby Boomers was published before we were even gleams in our parents' eyes: *The Great Gatsby*, the work of a talented, idealistic young man who let success go to his head and never quite fulfilled his early promise. Talk about cutting close to the bone.

In Georges Bernanos's bittersweet novel *The Diary of a Country Priest*, the doomed, cancer-ridden cleric who is the book's protagonist asks himself why it is that he has never been able to imagine what his life will be like when he is old. One day he visits a doctor and learns that he will be dead within months. Immediately, the scales drop from his eyes and he realizes that he had never been capable of envisioning himself as an old man because he was never going to be an old man. He was going to die before his thirtieth birthday. There was simply no old man in him.

Much the same can be said about my generation. We got off to a good start (the Freedom Riders, Woodstock, Four Dead in Ohio, driving Nixon from office, Jon Voigt in *Midnight Cowboy*). Then, John Lennon's death took the wind out of our sails. Gradually, we learned to prioritize, trade off synergies and interface, and we certainly did wonderful things with puff pastry. At the end of the day, the greatness expected of us never materialized, in part because we never stopped telling ourselves how great we were. Well, it's certainly not going to materialize now. The boys at Shiloh had that sense of achievement. The suffragettes had it. The Pilgrims had it. And my parents had it. Us? We talked a good game. But, to borrow Bernanos's phrase, we would never know what greatness felt like, because we had no greatness in us.

In the end, we were more like Cesar Cedeno, the flamboyant, fabulously talented Houston Astros center fielder who was called up to the majors in 1970 and was immediately anointed the next Willie Mays. Every spring, major sportswriters and announcers would be asked who they expected to win the batting title that year, and every year they would reply, "Cesar Cedeno."

Then, during the 1973 off-season, Cedeno was accused of voluntary manslaughter back home in Santo Domingo. Though the charges were eventually dropped, his game was never the same. His promise withered, and though he played until 1986, he ended his career batting .285 with 199 home runs, 976 RBIs, and 550 stolen bases. These are good numbers, but not great ones. They are the numbers posted by a gifted, ambitious man who started his career with immense promise, had some eye-opening achievements, but then tailed off. Cesar Cedeno was certainly not a flash in the pan. He was not an out-and-out bust. By no stretch of the imagination could he be dismissed as a dud. But in the end he did not deliver the goods. His youthful talent faded. The gods who had doted on him as a youth now turned their attention elsewhere. He did not end up a superstar batting .337, nor did he end up a mediocrity with a career batting average of .258. He ended up hitting .285, with some power to left-center field.

This is roughly the way history will view the Baby Boomers. They had immense youthful promise. They showed occasional flashes of genius. But poor judgment and a number of serious character flaws prevented them from achieving true greatness. They could have been contenders. But in the end, they didn't have what it takes. They ended up batting .285, which is perfectly good.

But it won't get you into Cooperstown.

Acknowledgments

When word got out that I was undertaking this Herculean project, the news spread like wildfire throughout the informal network of friends and associates I call my extended family. People I hadn't heard from in years began calling me at all hours of the night and day with anecdotes and reminiscences about the Age of Aquarius and the Eve of Destruction and the Me Decade and the Roaring Eighties. Because we only have one phone line in my house, there were many times they couldn't get through because my son was downloading God-knows-what off the Internet. Nevertheless, I am grateful for their enthusiasm.

There were also many e-mails and letters from dear old friends. Here is a typical example:

Dear The Queenans:

Wow! What a busy year it's been for the Padgett-Schwartzes! Emerson took second place at the Xtreme Yoga Gymnastics festival in San Francisco and Heath finished first in Manchurian Dung Quan Judo in Boston and second in Doi-Che-dong (a hybrid of yoga, boxing, ballet and karate) in Louisville. Meanwhile, Caitlin and Dakota got admitted to the John Hancock Summer Program for Preschoolers, even though we have not yet gone to China to formally adopt them. High fives all around! In the summer the whole clan went to the Lago di Como district on a tandem-bicycle marathon tour. While we were gone, Tilde, our nanny, was murdered by death squads in El Salvador. How weird is that??? The incident created a bit of a problem, because the kids had already gotten used to speaking Spanish and now they had to learn a whole new language, French, when we hired Chantal, who comes from Martinique. As luck would have it, Chantal was deported by the INS, but before she left she told us about a friend from Mexico, who is taking care of the kids now. Talk about life being like a box of chocolates! We're all crossing our fingers and hoping she doesn't die or get deported; it's been kind of rough on the little ones.

Barry's still doing his recidivist perp sensitivity training seminars while trying to get the underwater rock-climbing school up and running. Because so many insensitive people live in small towns in the Deep South, he's always flying on these little puddle-jumpers that totally freak him out. Last week we missed *Lord of the Dance* because he got stranded in Memphis. We ended up giving the tickets to Barry's parents, who hated it. Oh well, you can't teach an old dog a new trick. Or in this case, two dogs.

Speaking of dogs, Champignon and Misha got their pictures taken by *Silver Springs Spotlight*, and will appear in a feature about black Labs next month. Champignon was recently diagnosed with mandibular tendinitis; we took her to see a pet psychic to see how she felt about surgery, and she told the psychic she'd rather treat it herbally. Misha's best friend, Seleucid, the bull mastiff from down the street, passed away last week, and we've had Misha in bereavement counseling ever since. She's eating better now, and killing a few squirrels, but I think this one will take time.

Anyway, back to the kids. Last week we took Emerson and Dakota to see David Crosby. They haven't stopped talking about it since. As we were leaving, Emerson asked, "Mom, when did Raffi get so fat?" so I don't think she completely understood what was going on. But David was amazing; he sang "Wooden Ships," "Almost Cut Off My Hair" and "Guinevere," which was always my favorite. Next month, we're going to see Joni, who's playing on a triple bill with Joanie and Judy. No way I'm ready to hang up these rock 'n' roll shoes!

Don't forget to vote for Hillary,
The Padgett-Schwartzes

As this missive indicates, I got lots of support, which made my task much, much easier. In these pages, I have tried to the best of my ability to give voice to my generation, setting down on paper their ups, their downs, their highs, their lows, their ins, their outs, their whites, their blacks, their yings, their yangs. If I have failed in any way, I apologize in advance, as it is very unlikely that I will apologize once the book has been published.

In writing this book, I have received invaluable assistance from people too numerous to name. Nevertheless, I shall name all of them. If I have omitted anyone important, I am abjectly remorseful. But it is highly doubtful that I would forget anyone important, since these are the people best positioned to help me sell more copies of my book. Which is why I made a huge list of their names before I even started this project. If I have somehow managed to overlook someone who contributed to the writing of this book, they should take it as a pretty clear indication that neither their contribution nor their friendship is very highly valued, and stop reading right now.

Francesca Spinner, my wife of twenty-four years, has always been my north, my south, my east, my west, my polar star of India, my Aurora Borealis, my Tierra del Fuego, my touchstone, my watershed, my tipping point, my Rubicon, my Lethe, my Dardanelles, my Styx, my sine qua non, my friend and partner. Although it would be an exaggeration to say that she completes me, her presence in my life means that there is slightly more of me than there would be had we never met. In short, she partially completes me, which is better than nothing. To her I am eternally grateful, though 15 percent less eternally grateful than I am to my agent, Joe Vallely.

Martin Beiser, my friend and colleague at *GQ*, is the one who actually suggested that I write this book, though his ideas on how I should carry it out were almost completely useless, which is why I have basically ignored them. Through it all, Marty has supported me during the dark night of the soul when there were moments of terrible doubt. I have lost track of the number of times he made incisive suggestions as to how I could shape and organize my material, suggestions I ignored, because I hate it when people tell me what to do and because I was going to hear exactly the same long-winded spiel from my editor at Henry Holt anyway. Nevertheless, I am grateful for his spiritual and psychological support.

In researching the historical materials contained in this book, I am deeply indebted to Herodotus, Josephus, Thucydides, Plutarch, Julius Caesar, Cicero, Francis Parkman, Bernard De Voto, Arthur Schlesinger, Jr., Henry Steele Commager, Richard B. Morris, Allan Nevins, Stephen Ambrose, Pliny the Elder, Shelby Foote, Paul Johnson, David Frum, Charles and Mary Beard, Samuel Eliot Morrison, Winston Churchill, A. J. P. Taylor, J. M. Roberts, John Keegan, Bruce Catton, Alexis de Tocqueville and, of course, Edward Gibbon. In analyzing the whys and wherefores of my generation, I have drawn heavily on the works of Franz Kafka, Herman Hesse, Carlos Castaneda, Don Henley, Werner Heisenberg, Immanuel Kant, Sigmund Freud, David Brooks, Richard Brautigan, Joni Mitchell, Richard and Mimi Fariña, Frantz Fanon, Eldridge Cleaver, Angela

Davis, William of Ockham, Newt Gingrich, Neil Howe, William Strauss, Geraldo Rivera, Johannes Kepler, O. J. Simpson, John Duns Scotus and Dennis Miller. For help in finding *le mot juste*, which all too often eluded me, I shall forever be in the debt of Gustave Flaubert, Honoré de Balzac, Marcel Proust, Leo Tolstoy, Fyodor Dostoyevsky, Aeschylus, Euripides, Sophocles, Chaucer, Dante, Rabelais, Miguel de Cervantes, Molière, Jonathan Swift, George Bernard Shaw and Aristophanes, as well as Virgil, Ovid, Horace, Plautus, Terence, Jean Racine, Pierre Corneille, Alexander Pope, John Dryden, Samuel Johnson, Samuel Taylor Coleridge, John Keats, Percy Bysshe Shelley, Abbé Prévost, Madame de Staël, Herman Melville, Stephen Crane, Henry Miller, Ernest Hemingway, F. Scott Fitzgerald, H. L. Mencken, Mark Twain, William Faulkner, Flann O'Brien, Oscar Wilde, Sean O'Casey, John Millington Synge, Bram Stoker, Thomas Mann, Johann Goethe, Heinrich Heine, Georges Simenon, André Gide, Jean Giono, Samuel Beckett, Walter de la Mare, Charles Dickens, Charlotte Brontë, Jane Austen, William Thackeray, Italo Svevo, Ivan Turgenev, Junichiro Tanizaki, Yukio Mishima, Luigi Pirandello, Ignazio Silone, Roald Dahl, Mary Shelley, Voltaire, the guy who wrote *Cold Mountain* and, it goes without saying, William Shakespeare.

A book is not just about writing and research, not just about burning the midnight oil while the candle in the wind dwindles down to a precious few days at both sides now. A book is also about friendship and love. But even more than friendship and love it is about feeding an old friend some so-so material in the hope that he will mention you in the credits. Regardless of their motives, I am deeply indebted to Doug Colligan, Louise Colligan, T. J. Elliott, Tom Staudter, Gino Salomone, Chris Taylor, Rob Weiss, Jennifer Pradas, Carol Vinzant, Heidi Parker, Virginia Campbell, Jeff Nisbet, Hella Winston, Ben Olins, Kathy Sweeney, Diana Henriques, Leslie Eaton, Alan Abelson, Peter Newcomb, John Rezek, Raul Vega, Jill Rachlin, Art Cooper, Eliot Kaplan, Kathy Rich, Andy Ferguson and Howard Gold. I would also like to thank Susan Morrison, Dorothy Wickenden, Steve Reddicliffe, Kurt Andersen and Graydon Carter, none of whom actually helped in the writing of this book, but all of whom work for prestigious magazines where a kindly mention could help me move a lot of merchandise off the shelves. For similar reasons, I would like to thank Don Imus, David Letterman, Bill Maher, Michael Feldman, Terry Gross, Charlie Rose, Conan O'Brien and Jay Leno.

Finally, there is Agnes Catherine McNulty, without whose ministrations I would not even be here. First, I would like to thank her for her love. Next, I would like to thank her for her support. But mostly I would like to thank her for her timing. If my mother had given birth to me in 1965 or 1935, instead of 1950, I would now be writing a book about an entirely different generation, either the Beats or Gen X. This would be what was widely referred to in the halcyon salad days of my youth as "a drag."

Actually, if my mother had given birth to me in 1935, she would have only been fifteen, so the book probably would have been about growing up during the Depression with a single mother for a parent. In other words, more Frank McCourt–like whining: *Agnes's Ash Can*. Who needs that? All things considered, I'm grateful to my mother for bringing me into the world when she did.

Catering for this book was supplied by Bellas's Restaurant of Tarrytown, New York. Driving was supplied by my daughter, Bridget. My son, Gordon, ran a couple of useful errands. The accounting was handled by Charlie Snow.

As always, I am grateful to my editor, Jennifer Barth, for letting me keep as much of this material in the book as she has.